THE WAY OF FAITHFULNESS

THE WAY OF FAITHFULNESS
Contemplation and Formation in the Church

Padraic O'Hare

Trinity Press International   Valley Forge, PA

First Edition 1993

Trinity Press International
P.O. Box 851
Valley Forge, PA 19482-0851

Cover design: Jim Gerhard
Photo: Larry Fitzgerald

Library of Congress Cataloging-in-Publication Data

O'Hare, Padraic.
The way of faithfulness : contemplation and formation in the church / Padraic O'Hare.
p.   cm.
Includes bibliographical references and index.
ISBN 1-56338-066-8 : $13.50
1. Spirituality—Catholic Church. 2. Catholic Church—Education—United States. 3. Contemplation. 4. Faith development. 5. Spiritual formation.   I. Title.
BX1407.S66043   1993
248.3'4—dc20   93-22668
                                                                CIP

Printed in the United States of America.
93 94 95 96 97 98   6 5 4 3 2 1

Dedication

"A teacher is either a witness or a stranger"—
Rabbi Heschel

To
Gustavo Gutiérrez
and
Gabriel Moran
Teachers and Friends

Table of Contents

ACKNOWLEDGMENTS

Thanks are due to the following persons for assistance in the development of this book. Jane Brown, Edna Hess, Mike Callahan, Bernadette Kapner, Mildred (Shalom) Kutz, Jan Peregrine and Lynn Stenken, students at the Institute of Pastoral Studies, Loyola University of Chicago, for valuable suggestions made while using the pre-publication manuscript during a course on "Educating in Faithfulness," in Summer 1991.

Thanks to colleagues at Merrimack College, North Andover, Massachusetts, especially the members of the Faculty Senate Committee on Faculty Development Grants for a grant that underwrote work on portions of the book, and to Professors Art Ledoux and George Hoynacki for contributions to chapters 1 and 3.

To Maria Harris, Gabriel Moran, and Carol Ochs for reading the manuscript and making helpful suggestions as well as providing models of engaged scholarship. And to Michael St. Claire for continuing encouragement.

To William Neenan, S.J., Academic Vice President and Dean of Faculties at Boston College, for awarding me Visiting Scholar status at the university during academic year 1990-1991, a status which aided greatly in my research.

To Helen Earley for invaluable assistance in the preparation of this manuscript.

More broadly, I am indebted to a legion of teachers and

colleagues, within and outside the field of religious education, who have and continue to provide insight and needed inspiration. Among these are Joseph Carpino, Donald Gray, C. Ellis Nelson, John Rowan, Daniel Day Williams, Philip Phenix, Mary C. Boys, Thomas H. Groome, John Westerhoff, and Thomas Casey.

The notion of human faithfulness underlying this work is informed by the religious genius of Judaism. My own involvement in Jewish-Christian relations is for me the occasion for many clues about what it means to be faithful to the human vocation. So I am deeply indebted to Michael McGarry, C.S.P., who first introduced me to sustained Jewish-Christian conversation, and to Robert Bullock who serves as a continuing Christian model of that loving conversation; to Martin Goldman, Shiela Dectar, and Philip Perlmutter, friends and Jewish partners in dialogue. Above all, I am grateful for the friendship and witness of Rabbi Murray Rothman. Among many insights, Rabbi Rothman has taught me that "Life is a river," or maybe "it's not a river." And I give thanks for the persistent witness of Kathe McKenna of the Boston Catholic Worker.

Finally, I give thanks for Brian O'Hare and Margaret Ciski O'Hare. Though sublimely disinterested in the content of this book, they have nevertheless played an important role in its creation. If there is any wisdom in these pages, its discovery is inextricably linked to the lessons about human faithfulness that they continue to teach me.

Introduction

This book is about faithfulness, about living a faithful life, or what amounts to the same thing, striving to live a truthful life. Such a life would be one of "patient attentiveness and nonviolent receptiveness to what is real."[1]

This book is also about education, about the complex patterns of relationship between persons and within communities of persons through which we strive to be faithful, to learn faithfulness from others and to instill faithfulness in others, especially those for whom we care.

This book is about religious communities, communities of people which, for all their frailty, share some vision of the mystery of existence and of a way of life—a path of faithfulness or truthfulness—which is commensurate with that vision, that mystery.

Finally, this book is about contemplation, about cultivating a state of being, moment by moment, which is sufficiently peaceful that one is able to remain focused on the aim of a faithful or truthful life.

Of course, faithfulness, education, religious community, and contemplation can be understood in terms quite different from those set out here.

Faithfulness can be reduced to the "practice of religion" in a manner prescribed by the authorities of a religion acting according to their best lights to define orthodox belief and behavior.

Education can be reduced to training people to "practice religion," so that only those educational activities which promote a certain practice of religion—practice which authorities recognize as orthodox—are deemed appropriate religious education.

The richness of the religious community can be reduced to membership as proscribed by the authorities within a religion, so that only those who "practice religion" a certain way are understood as dutiful members. This delineation of what is and is not religious, who is and is not within the community, is often internalized, and persons accept the verdict that they are not faithful, do not build up faithfulness: in sum, are not in the community.

Finally, contemplation can be understood in a reductionistic way and therefore dismissed. If contemplation is understood as the luxury of people with vast amounts of time and few obligations, or as the temperamental option of essentially passive personalities, then holding out the aim of a contemplative way of being—a way to be moment by moment while engaged in all manner of activities—makes no sense for most of us.

This book proposes a different, integrative rather than reductionistic approach to faithfulness, education, community, and contemplation, for we must try to understand the common values in conflicting claims about what kind of life actually is faithful, educational, communal, and contemplative.

Faithfulness is never fully or adequately expressed in orthodox formulations of belief. Still, traditions of orthodoxy often preserve the memory of the way of faithful or truthful life lived by the founder and by adherents in earlier times.

Education is never fully served by instruction in an inherited content purporting to contain the answer to the question of faithfulness. Still, to the extent that traditions of orthodoxy *do* contain some of what has been called the "dangerous memories" of the way of the founder, instruction in belief is integral to education in faithfulness.

Truly religious communities are never identical to religious organizations. Still, elaborate religious institutions with a certain historical continuity—of existence if not always of teaching—are not, as sectarian Christianity would sometimes have it, merely the organized expression of unfaithfulness. The "officials" of a religious organization are sometimes the keepers of true faithfulness.

But choices must be made about how we educate and what kind of community we desire. These choices may not be "all or nothing" in character, but it would be naive to think that the choices that must be made entail nothing more than a strictly theoretical balance: "both/and." My primary interest is in "the way of faithfulness" within the Catholic Church in the United States and the choices to be made by the members of that religious community and by other Christian communities. And my primary thesis is this: where sustained, explicit, and vigorous (though gentle) efforts to form a contemplative people are a highly prized aim of the educators within the church, we will, as a people, choose faithfulness; we will not settle for what has been called "mere affirmation." We will choose education; we will not settle for instruction alone. We will choose community; organization will not satisfy us.

In a sense, this conviction is the same as that expressed by Saint Augustine, *"Lex orandi, lex credendi"*: "the law of prayer is the law of faith," or more recently by Gerald Sloyan, that the purpose of the church is to teach people how to pray.

Still, I have something quite explicit in mind in linking formation in the church to contemplation. I want every local religious community within the church to invite its members to engage in meditative practice in order—slowly, patiently, with ironic appreciation of how many steps backward each of us will inevitably take—to cultivate a contemplative mode of being. A state of being calm, collected, interiorly silent, present to each event moment by moment, ready; in a word, interiorly peaceful while calmly poised in the present moment for each new action. Only such a state of being enables a person to sustain a fundamental psychological posture of gratitude moment by moment, reverence for themselves and others and each evolving moment, that is reverence for time. Only the contemplative being can resist violence; only the contemplative being has the resources to create hospitable social environments in which this reverence, rather than violence, is lived.

The first task will be to consider contemplative being and meditative practice. Traditions of Western mysticism, both Christian and Jewish, together with insight from ancient Chinese religious philosophy and from Zen Buddhism, are brought together in an effort to designate with some specificity the psychological state constitutive of contemplative being. For those who appreciate the intimate relationship between Jewish and Christian religious worldviews and views of faithfulness, education, and community, little explanation for this mix is necessary. The introduction of insight about the meditative life from Taoist and Zen Buddhist sources may seem strange at first. However, the profound simplicity of these insights will shortly recommend them to the reader, provided I have not obscured their simplicity.

As to the propriety of this eclectic approach, even traditional Catholic Christians may be comforted by the words of the Vatican Council II document, *Ad Gentes*: "Christians must learn to assimilate the ascetical and contemplative traditions planted by God in ancient cultures prior to the preaching of the Gospel" (Paragraph 18).

In chapter 2, I will examine the conflicting claims regarding what faithfulness, education, and religious community truly are. This examination entails studying and understanding the message encoded in our roots: our Jewish roots, with their celebration of ordinary life, sanctification of time, and celebration of the wonder of creation, and the "true humanism," as Jacques Maritain termed it, of our Catholic and Christian roots. The examination of these sources and their messages encourages us to pay attention to the present time; in doing so we turn inevitably to the mode of practice that makes paying attention possible: meditation and the cultivation of contemplative being. Two thinkers, one a religious educator, the other a theologian, help in this work of retrieval of our roots in a special way. The substantial scholarly works of Gabriel Moran and Gustavo Gutierrez contain powerful and evocative expression of the path of faithfulness, education, and communality we must choose.

Chapter 3 is a nod to professional educators within the religious community, as well as to those true amateurs who read the literature of religious education and faith development, find it illuminating, and may wish to relate the aims of this book to these existing efforts to write about faithfulness, education, and community. Some of the most helpful analyses of Christian faithfulness in all its concreteness emanates from this literature. Though the review is not exhaustive, the ideas are assessed of some important and persuasive thinkers, including James Fowler, Maria Harris, Parker Palmer, Craig Dykstra, and John Westerhoff.

Chapters 4, 5, and 6 are an effort to connect contemplative formation to work and family life, to human religious development across the so-called life cycle, and to specific initiatives that local religious communities might take to engage in such formation. Chapter 4 is the most explicitly political essay in this volume. It identifies contemplative being as a form of resistance to alienating, brutal, or boring work. It is a plea to all educators within religious communities to arm adult workers with that sense of reverence for their work, their time, and themselves which enables them to resist being used or staying at destructive work. This resistance is associated with "contemplative irony"; it promises a revolutionary transformation in the work site.

Chapter 5 is an effort to trace the graces of a family environment characterized by contemplative freedom and nonviolence. Here the contemplative family is depicted as a "safe harbor" in which human beings can grow in "receptivity to self," children are respected, teenagers are affirmed during a natural period of uprootedness, and young adult self-assertion in pursuit of success is checked and balanced in gentle ways.

Chapter 6 is given over to suggestions for practical, concrete ways in which local religious communities might be places of contemplative formation or, as Gabriel Moran says, zones of quiet.

If, as Arthur Conan Doyle said, simplicity is genius, I can end this effort to explain the intent of *The Way of Faithfulness* on a note of genius by relating my intentions to two universal and simple Christian mantras. One appears throughout our scripture in slightly variant form: it is the prayer for "purity of heart." This book is an extended essay on how, in conceiving and practicing faithfulness, education, and community, we might be—as well as build up—a people with purity of heart. Perhaps even more simply put, this book is an effort to picture what Christian people might be—individually and collectively—if we could pray with utter sincerity and singlemindedness, "Come, Holy Spirit, and fill the hearts of the faithful."

Chapter One

"Treat Irritation [with] Compassion and Nonviolence": Contemplative Being

In light of the plurality that exists regarding the meaning and experience of mysticism, meditation, contemplation, prayer, mental prayer, prayerfulness, or the practice of the presence of God, let us begin with this functional definition of contemplative being: the state of contemplative being is approached when, as the Vietnamese Zen master Thich Nhat Hanh counsels, even irritation can be treated with compassion and nonviolence and be transformed.[1]

It is the goal of contemplative formation in the church to assist persons in achieving such a state of peaceful transformation of irritation, so that we may have a silent encounter with God and a nonviolent encounter with one another.

What follows is an eclectic profile of the contemplative state of being. "Contemplation" is employed not in a narrow, even technical sense, but broadly and generally as synonymous with a state of meditative calm and presence even amidst busyness. In this chapter I am less concerned with technique, with which chapter 6 will deal, than with the definition of this state of being and the qualities of behavior and of consciousness that constitute it.

The effort to describe what is common to many different mystical, meditative, or contemplative "ways," as well as to name a common set of emotional and behavioral outcomes such as calm and presence, peacefulness and gratitude, involves engaging very real theological and cultural differ-

ences. Ancient Buddhism does not contemplate God, for it
has no God; for this reason, in order that the Buddha not be
made a god, its ancient wisdom counsels "If you see the
Buddha, slay him." When the Taoist sage Chuang Tsu
speaks of sinking into Tao, he does not mean precisely what
Saint John of the Cross has in mind in being absorbed into
Nothing, *Nada*. The contemplative being depicted in the
utterly tranquil statue of a seated Buddha is not the same as
the rapture in Bernini's *Ecstasy of Santa Theresa*, with its utter
loss of self, the *unio mysticia* with God. This union is
expressed in the apophatic or negative (or "absorptive")
mysticism of Meister Eckhart, but is not so common in Jewish mysticism, although Moshe Idel has made a strong case
that there is a good deal more Kabbalistic, including Hasidic,
tradition than had previously been thought in which *devekut*
(union) is understood as real and radical assimilation or
"cleaving" in God.[2]

Despite differences, it is essential to name some common experiences, feelings, modes of consciousness, and
behaviors that are contemplative being: otherwise, efforts to
form a faithful people through contemplation will be dif-
fused. In the following pages we will see that common features of contemplative being can emerge from theologically
and culturally divergent paths.

CONTEMPLATIVE BEING

Thomas Merton says of contemplation: "[it] is the highest
expression of man's intellectual and spiritual life. It is that
life itself, fully awake, fully active, fully aware that it is
alive. It is spiritual wonder. It is spontaneous awe at the
sacredness of life, of being."[3] This "definition" reveals the
Eastern influence on Merton's thought, the references to
being "awake" and "aware" calling to mind the legend of
the first Buddha. Shakyamuni Buddha answered questions
about his nature from those overwhelmed by his person
and seeking a supernatural explanation by saying simply

that he was "awake." Merton's words also echo those of his friend Thich Nhat Hanh, whose writings are replete with the identification of enlightened life with being awake and aware, aware, for example, that I do not now have a toothache.

In Nhat Hanh's extraordinary commentary on Shakyamuni Buddha's "Sutra on the Full Awareness of Breathing," he relates the "Seven Factors of Awakening." First, practitioners are encouraged to pay *attention*. Second, we are directed to the work of *observation*, not in a detached mood but in order to contribute our attention to what is occurring. Such attention and observation generate *energy*, which enables us to encounter every feature of our experience with *lightness* and *peacefulness*. This concentration leads to *understanding*, or *prajna*. In Zen Buddhism, understanding is not identified with a content, a truth or truths to be known and affirmed, a "block of stuff," as is sometimes said. Understanding is a process through which "we can go beyond all comparing, measuring, discriminating and reacting with attachment and aversion." Finally there is *equanimity*, possession of which is attested by the practitioner's "bud of a half-smile, which proves compassion as well as understanding."[4]

Contemplative Being and Ego-Centeredness

Confronted with Merton's and Nhat Hanh's attractive picture of contemplative or meditative being, it is difficult to conceive why so few follow a disciplined and patient path to its achievement. To be fully awake, fully alive, fully aware, peaceful and therefore compassionate: who would choose to be asleep, bored and ignorant of the spirit's deepest yearnings, anxious and therefore aggressive? Yet, regretfully, as Kierkegaard says, "Man naturally loves finitude."[5] Establishing ourselves as the center of creation—ego-centeredness or what Augustine calls *hubris*—is the essential feature of humanity's tragic embrace of finitude. It is through contemplative practice that some element of infinity, expressing itself in "lives of compassion, joy and equanimity" (in the words of the Buddhist priest Sunyana Graef), is available to us.

Venerable Graef portrays the ruinous outcome of the ego-centered life in stark terms:

> Delusional thinking devolves from the ego, miring people in greed and jealousy, creating destructive emotions of hatred and anger and leaving a legacy of loneliness and pain. Most people are at the mercy of their bodies and mistaken beliefs, falling prey to neuroses and addictions in an attempt to palliate their emptiness.[6]

In Jewish and Christian traditions of prayerfulness, the essential function of contemplation is to center the human spirit in God through a stillness which overcomes, or at least mitigates, the destructive effects of ego-centeredness. Merton's discussion of contemplation continues along these lines: "[Contemplation] is a vivid realization of the fact that life and being in us proceed from an invisible, transcendent, infinitely abundant source. Contemplation is, above all, awareness of the reality of that Source."[7] Jewish theologian and rabbi Abraham Heschel, writing in the same vein, says:

> The self is not the hub, but the spoke of the revolving wheel. In prayer we shift the center of living from self-consciousness to self-surrender. God is the center toward which all forces tend. . . . Prayer takes the mind out of the narrowness of self-interest, and enables us to see the world in the mirror of the Holy.[8]

It may seem paradoxical that both Eastern and Western contemplative or meditative traditions invite us to look within and yet warn us about ego-centeredness. In much Eastern meditative tradition one is counseled to look within but also beyond the delusional self so easily scattered and dismayed by angry or jealous self- absorption. It is not Buddha who is within but one's own buddha mind! In Jewish and Christian traditions, we look for God within as well as without; God who is within but deeper within than sinful pride.

But the tendency of Western religion to lapse into harmful dualism and the caricature of Eastern spirituality as quietistic and socially unconcerned suggest caution in discussing contemplative being as overcoming ego-centeredness. Consider the prevailing superficial assessment of Buddhism, especially Zen Buddhism, with its erroneous idea that Buddhism encourages utter loss of self and withdrawal from the world. Thomas Merton, set upon revealing the spiritual richness of this tradition, repudiates this mistaken appraisal especially as applied to Zen:

> Zen insight is at once a liberation from the limitations of the individual ego, and a discovery of one's "original nature" and "true face" and "mind" which is no longer restricted to the empirical self but is in all and above all. [Zen] is not a pantheistic submersion or a loss of self in "nature" or "the One." It is not a withdrawal into one's spiritual essence and a denial of matter and the world. On the contrary it is a recognition that the whole world is aware of itself in me and that "I" am no longer my individual and limited self, still less a disembodied soul, but that my "identity" is to be sought not in that *separation* from all that is, but in oneness, (indeed convergence?) with all that is.[9]

The ego-centeredness which meditative and contemplative traditions seek to replace with steady, peaceful focus on the mystery of Being in which we participate is best understood as pride, as the earlier reference to Augustine implies. C. S. Lewis equated pride with hell: "We must picture Hell as a state where everyone is perpetually concerned about their own dignity and advancement, where everyone has a grievance, and where everyone lives the deadly serious passions of envy, self-importance and resentment."[10] Most meditative traditions counsel liberation from this personal hell that is the inevitable product of states of consciousness and styles of life which are not contemplative.

QUALITIES OF CONTEMPLATIVE BEING

The path to escape hell and embrace equanimity is one of simple practice leading to uncluttered consciousness. Meditation and contemplative being are one; the gentle practice and the state itself are the same. It is necessary, however, to speak of this state of being in analytic terms, and so a number of qualities will be examined. These qualities constitute what hereafter will be referred to simply as contemplative being—the presence or mindfulness which arises from concentration and leads to understanding, composure or calmness, and finally silence or stillness. The sum of these qualities is expressed as the "practice of the presence of God" in many Western traditions, and is described as emptiness—*Shunyata*—in the language of Eastern spirituality. After examining these qualities, we will turn to the moral substance of contemplative being, the "other side of the coin": compassion. The analysis will conclude with a discussion of the universal contemplative experience of "letting go" and the feelings of gratitude and thankfulness which this experience engenders.

Mindfulness

Monika Hellwig has a striking description of what she calls the "contemplative attitude"; her analysis underlines the quality of presence in contemplative traditions of East and West. She writes:

> The essence of a contemplative attitude seems to be vulnerability—allowing persons, things and events to be, to happen, allowing them their full resonance in one's experience, looking at them without blinking, touching them and allowing them to touch us without flinching. It is a matter of engaging reality in action, allowing it to talk back to us and listening to what is said. It is a constant willingness to be taken by surprise.[11]

The opposite of presence is absence. It is in presence, or being present "moment by moment" in a phrase often used by Zen masters, that the contemplative state consists. To be dragged back into the past or pulled forward into the future is to become scattered, ragged, dispersed. Christianity and Buddhism share a profound valuing of being present; in Christianity this practice of the presence of God is aided by the "Jesus prayer" or the prayer of his coming, "Maranatha." In Buddhism it is designated as the supreme quality of "mindfulness." The Taoist sage Chuang Tsu urges the true women and men of Tao to "keep [their] life collected in its own center."[12] Nhat Hanh says that "stopping and observing" (which he equates with concentration—*samadhi*—and understanding—*prajna*) are the only means of arriving at liberation, "the freedom from being bound."

> To what are we bound? First of all there is falling back into forgetfulness, losing our mindfulness. We live as if we are in a dream. We are dragged back into the past and pulled forward into the future. We are bound by our sorrows, by holding on to anger, by feelings of unease and fear. . . . "liberation" means going beyond and leaving these conditions behind in order to be fully awake, joyfully and freshly, at ease and in peace.[13]

The great Zen philosopher D. T. Suzuki echoes Nhat Hanh's profound psychological insight when he says of presence or mindfulness, "Unless 'was' and 'will be' turn into 'is' we cannot have peace of mind, we cannot escape dread."[14]

Distraction, dispersion, scatteredness are the opposite of presence or mindfulness; they are the source of unease and fear. They leave the mind incapable of concentration (stopping) and understanding (observing). The metaphor of the human mind as a band of crazed monkeys jumping madly from tree to tree is often invoked in Buddhist writings. Thomas Merton captures the depth of the problem when he notes that even "fun" has been despoiled for many in a world in which so much experience is inimical to contemplative being. In his essay "Rain and the Rhinoceros," Merton first addresses the quality of presence, just being

where one is, how one is, existing peacefully with no need
to be anywhere else or to escape presence by doing something:

> Can't I just be in the woods without any special reason?
> Just being in the woods, at night, in the cabin is some-
> thing too excellent to be justified or explained! It just *is*.
> There are always a few people who are in the woods at
> night, in the rain (because if there were not the world
> would have ended).[15]

Merton goes on to say that when he is in the woods in
this way, when he is truly present, he is not "having fun."
He is not having anything. "Having," with its connotation
of wanting which in turn suggests wishing that something
in the past could be undone or something in the future will
be just so, is the antithesis of the notion of presence and the
state of being which it embodies. Even fun is despoiled for
the person of scattered rather than present being. Play, of
which fun is surely a feature, is one of the human experiences of utter presence, an exhilarating focus on the vitality
and richness of the moment. But unless one's being is contemplative, Merton assures us fun becomes "a state of dif-
fuse excitation that can be measured by the clock and
stretched by an appliance."[16]

A Zen poem captures the state of being, the gentle
mode of effort (or practice) and the moral and psychological
benefits of presence or mindfulness. The poet counsels us:

> Be a bud sitting quietly in the hedge
> Be a smile one part of wondrous existence
> Stand here, there is no need to depart
> This homeland is as beautiful as the homeland
>   of your childhood
> Do not harm it, please
> And continue to sing.[17]

By presence or mindfulness awe becomes possible; it
becomes possible to be "vulnerable to" our experience, surprised by it. Noting the commonly expressed idea that

humans come from dust and will return to dust, Nhat Hanh goes so far as to say that for the mindful person "to return to a speck of dust will be quite an exciting adventure."[18]

Presence or mindfulness is wisdom, but many Buddhist scholars, as noted earlier, do not wish to translate *prajna* as wisdom, preferring the word "understanding." They wish to avoid associating wisdom with content, with an unmoved block of truth. Better to think of wisdom or understanding as something that flows, as process, than as a kind of "conceptual" substance.

The same insight concerning the process of understanding appears in John O'Hara's novel, *Appointment in Sumara*. O'Hara repeats the Muslim tale of the man who flees to Sumara because he has a vision that the angel of death will come for him; the angel of death reports in a conversation that he is bound for Sumara. Similarly, a Buddhist tale speaks of a man who learns of the death of his infant son, though the son has not in fact died. When the son is an adult he makes several efforts to present himself to his perpetually grieving father but the father, having a "truth" that his son died in infancy, never responds. The same insight about the illusory character of truth as a content, a body of sure wisdom, is behind Oscar Wilde's famous aphorism that only two tragedies exist: not getting what one wants and getting what one wants. George Bernard Shaw makes the same point when he says that two games are always being played in human relations: the one we are playing and the one that is being played.

Another way of stating this idea is to say that wisdom or understanding is "readiness." The person who is contemplative in being, present and mindful, is ready. Ready, moment by moment, each moment. The twentieth-century Zen monk Shunryu Suzuki says of this quality that, for one who is ready, each and every experience is recognized as if it were the face in the mirror. The emphasis on presence in its aspect of readiness is, of course, highly functional; there really are, after all, only two states of being: ready and unready. Thus Suzuki Roshi speaks from a very practical point of view: "Our teaching is just to live always in reality in its exact sense. To make our effort, moment after moment, is our way. In an exact sense, the only thing we actually can study in our life is that on which we are working in each moment."[19] But readiness is not merely instrumental, an exercise enabling us to do something well resulting from paying attention. Readiness is wisdom itself, profound wisdom, the only wisdom: . . . the readiness of the mind . . . is wisdom . . . wisdom is not something to learn. Wisdom is something that will come out of your mindfulness. . . . the point is to be ready for observing things and to be ready for thinking.[20]

In recounting the story of Bodhidharma, the great Zen master of the sixth century c.e., D. T. Suzuki supplies a personal image of readiness as wisdom. Bodhidharma is commanded to appear before the emperor and the court to undergo sharp questioning with danger in miscalculation. He is summoned, in other words, to a prototypical situation of potential anxiety, fear, irritation, anger, and scatteredness. But Bodhidharma is enlightened, he is a contemplative being; he is ready. He is, in D. T. Suzuki's words, "absolutely free of all bondage and will not be lead astray because of linguistic complication": "Bodhidharma's emptied mind had no premeditated measures, no calculating plans. He just acted in the freest manner possible cutting everything asunder that would obstruct his seeing directly into Nature in its entire nakedness."[21]

The Christian parallel is to pray without ceasing for the coming of the Holy Spirit. Jesus' counsel to his followers when they are in circumstances like those in which Bodhidharma finds himself is strikingly similar:

> When they deliver you up, do not be anxious how you are to speak or what you are to say; for what you are to speak will be given to you in that hour; for it is not you who speak, but the Spirit of your Father speaking through you. (Mt. 10:19-20)

This same valuation of the contemplative quality of presence and readiness each moment is celebrated in Jewish spirituality in cultivating a sense of the sacredness of time— its holiness, as Genesis says. Rabbi Abraham Heschel addresses this contemplative dimension when he writes:

> The passage of hours is either an invitation to despair or a ladder to eternity. This little time in our hands melts away ere it can be formed. Before our eyes, man and maid, spring and splendor, slide into oblivion. However there are hours which perish and hours that join the everlasting. Prayer is a crucible in which time is cast in the likeness of the eternal. Humans hand over our time to God in the secrecy of single words. When anointed by prayer, a person's thoughts and deeds do not sink into nothingness, but merge into the endless knowledge of an all-embracing God. We yield our thoughts to God who endowed us with a chain of days for the duration of our lives.[22]

Western Christian mystical tradition contains the same identification of blessedness with presence. Meister Eckhart says that "the soul who is in the present now, in her the Father bears his once-begotten Son and in that same birth the soul is born back into God."[23] And Thomas Merton, praying for presence, says, "If I were looking for God, every event, every moment would sow in my will grains of [God's] life that would spring up one day in a tremendous harvest."[24]

Thus, contemplative being is present or mindful being; only gentle practice, persisting moment by moment, will open this way of being to us. It is achieved through stopping and observing, understood as concentration and understanding. The stopping and observing are, in themselves, freedom or liberation from what binds us. In the traditional religious language of the West, this quality enables us to live each moment of time as "sabbath time." When we try to live this way, moment by moment, we make of our lives, in the words of D. T. Suzuki, "an inimitable masterpiece, [for] every minute of human life as long as it is an expression of its inner self is original, divine, creative, and cannot be retrieved. Each individual life is thus a great work of art."[25]

Composure

Presence, or mindfulness, is experientially indistinguishable from composure, or calmness. The distinction is made here for the purpose of analyzing a mode of consciousness which is by definition unitary. In his groundbreaking study, *Zen Catholicism*, the Benedictine Dom Aelred Graham says that the necessary predisposition for the practice of Zen is the state of being "calm, controlled, quiet, patiently enduring and content."[26] Chuang Tsu counsels, "Hold your being secure and quiet; keep your life collected in its own center. Do not let anything disturb your thoughts."[27] And at the beginning of his book, *Being Peace,* Nhat Hanh recounts a story involving one of the children who reside with him at Plum Village outside of Paris.[28] Having played with children who came to the village as guests, the child asks "Uncle Monk," as she calls Nhat Hanh, for a drink for herself and the others. Nhat Hanh gives them apple juice and reminds the resident child to let the guests drink first. However, since the juice is fresh, the last glass of juice has pulp floating in it, and the little child who is serving as host does not want to drink it. She leaves with the other children, mildly upset at Uncle Monk for reminding her to take refreshment only after her guests. Later the child returns, sees that the pulp in the glass has all settled—calmly—at the bottom of glass. She drinks the apple juice with pleasure. Still later, at meditation in the evening, the child asks Uncle Monk if their meditation isn't a bit like the pulp gently resting at the bottom of the glass. With this story, Nhat Hanh invites us to take up the life of meditative composure and calm.

Composure and calmness are products of the contemplative way of being that allow us to greet even irritation, anger, and jealousy with peace. They are, as well, the basis of that concentration which is associated with mindfulness and the wisdom—as understanding—which flows from it. Shunryu Suzuki speaks eloquently of these qualities:

> The important thing in our understanding is to have a smooth, free thinking way of observing. We have to think and to observe things without stagnation. We should accept things the way they are without difficulty. Our mind should be soft and open enough to understand things as they are. When our thinking is soft and open enough it is called imperturbable thinking. This kind of thinking is always stable. . . . Concentration should be present in our thinking. . . . Whether you have an object or not your mind should be stable and your mind should not be divided.[29]

The great enemy of the concentrated mind, and therefore of contemplative being itself, is the mind made ragged by busyness. Only composure or calmness can liberate the mind from this corrosive busyness. Shunryu Suzuki continues:

> If you become too busy and too excited, your mind becomes rough and ragged. This is not good. If possible, try to be always calm and joyful and keep yourself from excitement. Usually, we become busier and busier, day by day and year by year, especially in our modern world. . . . It cannot be helped. But if we become interested in some excitement, or in our own change, we will become completely involved in our busy life, and we will be lost. But if your mind is calm and constant, you can keep yourself away from the noisy world even though you are in the midst of it. In the midst of noise and change, your mind will be quiet and stable.[30]

Chuang Tsu writes with equal power about the self-destructive pursuit of raggedness and irritation found in feverish and often gratuitous activity which prevents calmness from taking root in the human spirit. Like Shunryu Suzuki, who associates unlimited possibilities with preserving "beginner's mind" but limited possibilities with the mind of the expert, Chuang Tsu also identifies raggedness and the loss of composure with the pride and pursuits of the experts:

> If an expert does not have some problem to vex him, he is unhappy! If a philosopher's teaching is never attacked, he pines away! If critics have no one on whom to exercise their spite, they are unhappy. . . . He who wants followers seeks political power. He who wants reputation seeks an office. The strong man looks for weights to lift. The brave man looks for an emergency in which he can show his bravery. The swordsman wants a battle in which he can swing his sword. Men past their prime prefer a dignified retirement in which they may seem profound. Men experienced in law seek difficulty. . . . Liturgists and musicians like festivals in which they may parade their ceremonious talents. The benevolent, the dutiful, are always looking for chances to display virtue. . . . All such men are prisoners in the world of objects. . . . they have no choice but to submit to the demands of matter! They are pressed down and crushed by external forces, fashion, the market, events, public opinion. Never in a whole lifetime do they discover their right mind! The active life! What a pity![31]

Yet it should not be assumed from these references to calmness that contemplative being is passive and disengaged. Nhat Hahn has said concerning the activity of the comtemplative:

> We walk all the time, but usually it is more like running. When we walk like that, we print anxiety and sorrow on the Earth. We have to walk in a way that we only print peace and serenity on Earth. Everyone of us can do that provided that we want it very much. Any child can do that. If we can take one step like that, we can take two, three, four and five. When we are able to take one step peacefully, happily, we are for the cause of peace and happiness for the whole of humankind.[32]

The intimate relationship between contemplation and action will be addressed later in this chapter and throughout the rest of the book. For now, Merton's cogent disclaimer will do:

> . . . contemplation is not just the affair of a passive and quiet temperament. It is not mere inertia, a tendency to inactivity, to psychic peace. The contemplative is not merely a man who likes to sit and think, still less one who sits around with a vacant stare.[33]

Mindfulness, in these aspects of presence, composure, calmness, is linked intimately to the physiological discipline of breathing gently, deeply, rhythmically. Such practice is acknowledged as crucial in *Dikr*, the meditation practice of Sufi Muslems, as well as in the "centering prayer" of Christians. In Zen Buddhism, as well, such practice is understood as crucial to well being and to compassionate being. Commenting on Buddha's "Sutra on the Full Awareness of Breathing," Nhat Hanh writes:

> Our mind can be tied up by sorrows and memories of the past; or drawn along by anxieties and predictions concerning the future; or held subservient to feelings of irritation, fear and doubt in the present; or obscured and confused by inaccurate perceptions. Only by concentrating the mind do we have the capacity to observe and illumine and be emancipated from obstacles. It is the same as when we try to take knots out of thread. We have to be calm, and we need to take time. By observing our mind in all its subtlety, in a calm and self- contained way, we can free our mind from all confusion.[34]

We will have more to say of breathing discipline in chapter 6. For now, consider one more effort to capture this quality of mindfulness or presence, with its fruits of composure and calmness. Again, it comes from Nhat Hanh, as he writes:

> Mindfulness is the miracle by which we master and restore ourselves. Consider, for example: a magician who cuts his body into many parts and places each part in a different region—hands in the south, arms in the east,

legs in the north—and then by some miraculous power
lets forth a cry which reassembles whole every part of his
body. Mindfulness is like that—it is the miracle which can
call back in a flash our dispersed mind and restore it to
wholeness so that we can live each minute of life.[35]

Meister Eckhart refers to this same quality as "purity of
heart," for which Christians pray when they call upon the
Holy Spirit to come and fill their hearts. May we gently
strive to cultivate a state of being of such contemplative calm
that Eckhart's prayer might come true in our minds—that is,
our hearts, our selves: "Blessed are the pure of heart who
leave everything to God, now as they did before ever they
existed."[36]

Silence

In addition to mindfulness or presence, and the fruit of composure and calmness, another equally rich way of expressing the essence of contemplative being is found in
considering this state as one of silence or stillness. Here
again, Meister Eckhart is instructive: "In all creation there is
nothing so like God as stillness."[37] To be silent is to be lost
in God. Or, as Chuang Tsu says, to be silent, to be still, is to
be a true woman or man of Tao:

> The heart of the wise man is tranquil. It is the mirror of
> heaven and earth. The glass of everything. Emptiness,
> stillness, tranquility, tastelessness, silence, non-action,
> this is the level of heaven and earth. This is perfect Tao.
> Wise men find here their resting place. Resting, they are
> empty. . . . From the sage's emptiness, stillness arises.
> From stillness, action. From action, attainment. From their
> stillness comes their non-action, which is also action. And
> is, therefore, their attainment. For stillness is joy. Joy is
> free from care, fruitful in long years. Joy does all things
> without concern: for emptiness, stillness, tranquility,
> tastelessness, silence and non-action are the root of all
> things.[38]

Quaker wisdom has much the same lesson to teach us about cultivating silence. Parker Palmer speaks from this tradition:

> The ultimate lesson silence has to teach us is that God and the world have not absented themselves from us—we have absented ourselves from them. We have hidden behind the barriers of impersonal knowledge because we do not want to be found out. The knowing self is full of darkness, distortion and error; it does not want to be exposed and challenged to change. It seeks objectified knowledge in order to know without being known. If we can learn this lesson from the discipline of silence, we will be led into the discipline of solitude where this evasive knowing self can be brought out of hiding to be transformed by truth and love.[39]

The great Protestant theologian Paul Tillich also speaks of the importance of silence, saying that in moments of silent solitude "something is done to us. The center of our being, the innermost self that is the ground of our aloneness, is elevated to the divine center and taken into it."[40] Catholic theologian Karl Rahner is equally eloquent on the subject of silence. In his small masterpiece, *Encounters with Silence*, Rahner prays:

> I now see clearly that if there is a path at all on which I can approach you, it must lead through the middle of my ordinary life. . . . But doesn't [ordinary life] immerse me all the more deeply in the empty noise of worldly activity, where you, God of Quiet, do not dwell? . . . Without you I should founder helplessly in my own dull and groping narrowness. I could never feel the pain of longing . . . had not my mind again and again soared out over its limitations into the hushed reaches which are filled by you alone, the Silent Infinite.[41]

Rabbi Abraham Heschel speaks for a tradition of Jewish mysticism when he asks: "Is not listening to the pulse of wonder worth silence and abstinence from self-assertion? Why do we not set apart an hour of living for devotion to

God by surrendering to stillness? We dwell on the edge of mystery and ignore it, wasting our souls and risking our stake in God."[42]

Emptiness

If "stillness" designates the contemplative state by employing an auditory image, "emptiness" is the spatial metaphor for contemplative being. Emptiness, or for Buddhists *Shunyata*, is a universal category employed across religious traditions to express the essence of contemplative being. It is emptiness to which Saint Paul points when he speaks of Christ living in him, and to which Meister Eckhart refers in his well-known image of the soul of such poverty that God has not a place within them. Speaking of the Buddhist meaning, D. T. Suzuki says:

> Buddhist emptiness . . . is Absolute Emptiness transcending all forms of mutual relationship, of subject and object, birth and death, God and the world, something and nothing, yes and no, affirmation and negation. In Buddhist emptiness there is no time, no space, no becoming, no-thing-ness; it is what makes all things possible; it is the zero full of infinite possibilities, it is the void of inexhaustible contents.[43]

The idea that contemplative being is empty being is at first almost impossible for the Western mind to entertain. Fullness of being would be more to our liking; the phrase contains more cultural resonance for materially prosperous peoples. Thus we struggle to grasp the truth of *Prajnaparamita Sutra*, the classic Buddhist sutra dealing with the perfect understanding that everything (form or body, feelings, perceptions, mental formations, and consciousness) is empty. In his commentary on the sutra, Nhat Hanh makes a strikingly clear and compelling effort to explain the profound simplicity of the teaching. To be, to be there, to be available, to be free, is to be empty.

The word emptiness should not scare us. It is a wonderful word. To be empty does not mean to be nonexistent. . . . Emptiness is the ground of everything. Thanks to emptiness everything is possible. . . . If I am not empty, I cannot be here. And if you are not empty, you cannot be there. . . . If we are not empty, we become a block of matter. We cannot breathe, we cannot think. To be empty means to be alive, to breathe in and breathe out. We cannot be alive if we are not empty.[44]

CONTEMPLATIVE BEING AND COMPASSION

The discussion of contemplative being as emptiness is a useful bridge to considering the relationship between compassion and contemplation. Toxic wastes such as irritation, anxiety, fear, anger, jealousy, envy, and ego-centeredness fill the mind (which is to say, the heart or the self). In the Christian tradition's Seven Deadly Sins, or Buddhism's nine *Samyojana* (desire, hatred, pride, ignorance, stubborn view, doubt, attachment, jealousy, and selfishness), we have revealed the blocks to compassion for other human beings and nonhuman elements in life. If emptiness is the fruit of contemplation, then this emptiness is the key to the experience of oneness with all of creation and therefore the means for removing blockages to compassion. This is what Merton means when he decries the misleading association of Zen with self-centered detachment rather than the proper interpretation that for Zen identity is found in oneness, not separation.

The truly contemplative being is not "some private entity traveling unaffected through time and space as if sealed off from the rest of the world by a thick wall."[45] What one is emptied of in contemplation is selfish desire. For Shakyamuni Buddha, desire is the cause of all suffering; for Augustine, misdirected desire is the basis of pride. Pride leads to exaggerated and destructive individualism, but since we are not made for such individualism, it inevitably induces anxiety and requires aggression. To be empty, on the other hand, is to be available for compassion. As Sunyana Graef says, "it is what we *do not* have—self-centeredness, immaturity, greed and anger—that enables us to live a compassionate life full of peace and freedom."[46]

The emptiness of contemplation is the source of compassion because this emptiness enables us to be a part of a larger whole and to perceive ourselves as such. The whole may be spoken of as "The Great Chain of Being," "Tao," or the "Mystical Body of Christ." However these terms differ in meaning, functionally a contemplative and compassionate life is lived in the belief that

> . . . we are only alive when we live the life of the world, and so live the joys of others. The suffering of others is our own suffering and the happiness of others is our own happiness. . . . Having seen the reality of interdependence and entered deeply into its reality, nothing can oppress you any longer. You are liberated.[47]

A most dramatic example of the Zen Buddhist tradition linking enlightenment with compassion is given by the Japanese master Taisen Deshimaru in his discussion of the Bodhisattva. The image of the Bodhisattva is of a Buddha who, having achieved enlightenment, remains among women and men instead of slipping quietly into the extinguishment of Nirvana in order to teach the way of enlightenment or being awake. This is the ultimate expression of compassion, to postpone one's own "salvation," to put it in a Western perspective. Deshimaru Roshi speaks of compassion as a willingness to "jump into hell":

> The Zen monk must leap into hell to save those who are suffering. The Bodhisattva must leap into the impurities of the social world. Leap, not fall! Falling into the river and diving into the river are completely different things. If you fall into the river your only thought is to save your life. If you dive into the river you swim and then you can save people who are drowning. Bodhisattvas dive into the world to help.[48]

Johannes Metz's idea of the "mysticism of fraternity" (despite dramatically gender-exclusive language) reveals the same link between the contemplative inner life and the compassionate social life: though "in our mind [mysticism] is generally connected with distance from men and the world and easily acquires for us the character of the subjective and the private," Metz assures us:

> Christian mysticism is neither a kind of pantheistic infinity mysticism nor an esoteric mysticism of exaltation, tending toward the self-redemption of the individual soul. It is rather . . . a mysticism of fraternity. . . . Christian mysticism finds . . . that direct experience of God it seeks precisely in daring to imitate the unconditional involvement of the divine love for man.[49]

Perhaps the final word on the relationship between contemplation and compassion is this simple expression from Meister Eckhart: "What a man takes in by contemplation he must pour out in love."[50]

CONTEMPLATIVE BEING AND GOD

It bears repeating that while not all the traditions to which reference has been made in this effort to describe contemplative being are theistic, the purpose of this book is to promote formation in Christian faithfulness through contemplative practice—in this context, encountering God through a steady state of prayerfulness is contemplative being. As Paul Tillich said of Meister Eckhart's mystical teachings, "To receive the divine substance, serenity or patience, no moving is needed. Eckhart fought against making the religious relationship a matter of purposing."[51] And Eckhart himself states, "There, where clinging to things ends, God begins to be."[52] Eckhart's theological work provided not only for "God," but, behind God, "Godhead," and the insight is shared by Rabbi Heschel, who says, "to pray means to bring God back into the world, to establish God's Kingdom for a second at least. To pray means to expand God's presence."[53] When, through contemplative being, we are present to God's presence, consciousness is suffused, moment by moment, with surprise, gratefulness, and thanksgiving. It is for this reason that Eckhart says that if all we ever pray is "thank you," it is enough, and Rabbi Heschel insists that the preeminent virtue for the Jew is awe.

In *Gratefulness, the Heart of Prayer*, Brother David Steindl-Rast employs a good deal of the poetry of Rilke. One of these poems is especially suggestive of the relationship between contemplation, thanksgiving, and the experience of the presence of God:

> Oh, if for once all were completely still!
> If all mere happenstance and chance
> were silenced, and laughter next door, too;
> if all that droning of my senses
> did not prevent my being wide awake
> Then, with one thousandfold thought,
> I would reach your horizon
> and, for the span of a smile, hold you
> to give you away to all life
> as thanksgiving.[54]

The contemplative state is a way of faithfulness for which many of us yearn and sorely desire to explore more deeply. But we may well ask whether prevailing patterns of religious formation within the church, as well as the institutional self-understanding of its role which church leaders possess, support such contemplative formation. It is to this question that we turn in the next chapter.

Chapter Two

"To Celebrate Life's Joys and Bear with its Sorrows": The Way of Faithfulness and Ecclesial and Educational Patterns

Members of a faith community inspired with yearning for contemplative being will seek to establish patterns of formation in faithfulness to achieve this contemplative purpose. These patterns of formation in faithfulness are rightly called "religious education", despite the temptation to employ "religious education" in a narrow and reductionist manner and to find some other phrase for efforts to promote faithfulness. Consider Thomas Groome's powerful definition of religious education:

> Education that is intentionally "religious" is clearly a transcendent activity. In attempting to "bring things together again" (a meaning suggested by the Latin roots of *religious*) in the context of ultimacy, it attempts to nurture to awareness and lived expression the human capacity for the transcendent. In other words, [religious education] encourages people to interpret their lives, relate to others, and engage in the world in ways that faithfully reflect what they perceive as ultimate in life, that is, from a faith perspective.[1]

The call for religious education that induces the members of the faith community to live and to act in accord with loyalty to what is experienced as ultimate is a call for education that confronts what is real. I will have more to say about the "Real" framed as a problem of the philosophy of knowledge (epistemology) in chapter 3. Here, I mean to point to what really induces faithfulness, to what really moves the heart. In this view of religious education, changing or moving the heart, the whole person in her or his real life and patterns of relationship, is the goal. It is interesting to note that *credo*, the Latin word for faith so often translated "I believe," actually means "to give one's heart."[2]

Historical developments, cultural patterns, and church structures both advance and retard religious education that confronts what is real. In contemporary Catholic Christianity, faithfulness to what is real is promoted by the emphases on experience, on liturgical formation, on the church as a community of disciples, on the ultimate claims that the poor and their right to justice and peace make on us. When, however, experience is invoked to escape the discipline of life in a faith community, when liturgy continues along "routinized" and hollow lines, and where authoritarian restoration is the order of the day, faithfulness is diminished and hearts are not moved.

We need to take our bearings: what values and attitudes are faithful, what patterns of formation are real and move the heart? In this chapter I propose to look at these questions from four perspectives: the religious educational thought of Gabriel Moran; the theological thought of Gustavo Gutiérrez; the life-giving example of Judaism; and the ambiguities of culture and church structure, including the elemental value at the heart of the Catholic ethos that is the essential Catholic spirit.

At every point in this analysis we are reminded of the truth that forming ourselves as a contemplative people is the key to faithfulness. In Moran's thought the contemplative values of waiting and presence, attentiveness, nonviolence, and gratitude are emphasized. He presents the ideals of professional activity within the faith community that is free of the obsession to control, of education as concern for the ordinary lives we live, of human development as culminating in "centering," with centered being and compassion indivisible.

In Gutiérrez's thought we are cautioned not to make a "theology" the end of Christian life. Holiness is held up as the essence of active and morally responsible faithfulness, and attentiveness to the "tenth hour" in each of our lives as the key to freedom. For Gutiérrez, silence is the ground of a faithful community.

Many of these themes are reiterated from a fresh perspective in the section on Judaism, for much of what is proposed by Gutiérrez and Moran is actually a "re-Judaizing" of Christianity.

In the final section of this chapter, conflicting trends in education, culture, and church life will be examined. This represents a cautionary tale, for much in education, culture, and church life is inimical to contemplative being, to real faithfulness. Yet I believe that a way of faithfulness wholly linked to contemplative formation is to be found in retrieving and renewing the Catholic spirit, a spirit which is not second- hand or controlling, caught up with fears for orthodoxy or order. This spirit, like contemplative being and the life it encourages, is a matter, as Rahner says, of "letting myself sink into incomprehensible mystery."

GABRIEL MORAN AND PATTERNS OF EDUCATION

Religious education is a way to help people "celebrate life's joys and bear with its sorrows."[3] Such education "begins by naming the ways people live and then it attempts to give them a richer communal meaning for working out their lives."[4] These words typify Gabriel Moran's efforts over thirty years to encourage those who would build a faithful community to see before they speak, to name what is there before prescribing what is to be done. It is Moran more than anyone else who has insisted that professionals within the faith community honor the richness of the many educational processes which are occurring in people's lives, to honor what is real. This plea has usually taken the form of a caution not to identify all the educational influences within a faith community with the single form of education involved in schooling.

An important aspect of Moran's advice is his analysis of professionalization and its ambiguities. He manages to level the criticism without, however, calling into question the many gains that this process has wrought in the life of the faith community. Moran contrasts the pre-modern and modern function of the professional:

> In the pre-modern form, the professional lived in the community and served it on a permanent basis. In the modern meaning there is a "professional community" which supplies individuals to local communities on a temporary basis. . . . In pre-modern times the professional accepted his/her knowledge as a grace to be shared; the community granted "license" to this person's challenging the community. In its modern form the professional's knowledge and status give a protected status: the community is not allowed to intrude.[5]

Concerning the relationship between education and schooling, Moran writes: "Education is a different kind of reality from school and schooling . . . Education is . . . a lifetime process constituted by a set of relations. . . . Education is reshaping life's forms. . . . It is careful response to what living (and its inevitable associate dying) presents to us."[6] Thus, to put it in contemplative terms, the purpose of religious education is to learn to live the "truthful" life. Moran speaks about the truthful life in a way which reveals the Eastern influence on his thought: as "a lifetime of patient attentiveness and nonviolent receptiveness to what is real."[7]

For Moran there is a providential, though not inevitable, pattern of religious education occurring in four movements in the communal lives of people: the acknowledgment of the gifts of ordinary life; the realization that the ordinary lives we live are not the only ordering of life; the reach to transcend the ordinary world (which is always rooted in appreciation of the ordinary joys and sorrows of life[8]); and the actual achievement by individuals and groups of lives of more careful response, more compassionate "reshaping," more truthful lives.

The religious educator is the companion and helper in this process; she or he is at once a catalyst nurturing deeper appreciation and more "careful response" to the gifts of ordinary life, and someone within the community who calls it beyond the present order to deeper levels of compassion, justice, and inclusion. Moran is convinced that when the members of a faith community pay careful attention to reshaping everyday life in its most concrete and specific aspects they grow in faithfulness.

For Moran, the community continually reshapes itself in order to become more simple, less violent, less noisy, less wasteful, less isolated, and more grateful for food and energy and friendship and diverse other gifts. Moran believes that when a faith community forms itself along these more truthful lines it becomes a "school" of empathy and respect and compassion for all other people's communities. He says:

> To accept life in a community is implicitly an affirmation of life itself. It is a recognition that this people that I call my people is an embodiment of the universal human community. . . . Every religious community is a protest against or resistance to some force of death or destruction.[9]

Moran's Four Social Forms

An important element in Moran's vision of religious education, one which demands that professionals let go of undue preoccupation with programmatic initiatives and pay more attention to the lives of people within the community, is his identification of four social forms within which education occurs: family, school, job, and leisure. Each mode of human practice and form of human relationship is as potentially powerful an educational influence as the other, but there is an obvious imbalance between the institutional pri-

ority placed on "schooling" in religion within the church
and the relatively modest priority assigned the promotion of
religious education as it occurs within family life, through
work, and at leisure. It isn't that schooling in all its many
expressions is diminished in importance in Moran's
thought. Rather, in pointing to the importance of all four
educational patterns of relationship and the faithfulness
they induce, Moran is insisting on a radical shift and a new
educational agenda in the church. In his view, the educational practice of the church must serve not only schooling
functions but also the need for intimate community (family),
salvation from violent and brutalizing labor (work), and contemplative silence and creative aging (leisure).

Moran believes that each social form embodies a "universal value," though each also reveals a tension "between
partial embodiment and universal value."[10] (In this aspect I
believe his thought expresses a Catholic theology of grace,
as I hope to make clear later in this chapter.) Family is the
form for the growth of community; it serves the universal
value of "communion." School is the form especially well
designed to provide knowledge which results in the universal value "vision." Job is the form where true work should
occur, nurturing the universal value "vocation." And leisure, for young and old, is the source of contemplative
silence from which "wisdom" may spring.

Moran's call is for a response on the part of the faithful
community to the actual lives we lead. It is a call to serve the
familial, work, and contemplative needs of our people with
the same zeal and at the same levels of institutional commitment with which—goaded by the power our own message
has over us—we presently attempt to serve real and imag-
ined needs for knowledge of religion and religious practice.
Yet, in the Catholic Church at least, little is currently being
done through institutional and programmatic forms and
structures to nurture communality, workmanship, and
silence in family, worksite, and leisure. Consider the epi-
demic of violent and fragmented families, hopeless and bru-

tal labor, and exhausting "recreation," to which little formal church programming responds. We can be grateful for the increasing numbers of professional persons within the faith community who do in fact rest their efforts on a clear-sighted appraisal of real human need and the social forms within which these needs express themselves. But the greater share of time and money, institutional assets, and human labor in the church go to one or another form of schooling in religion, designed to communicate a message— all of it founded on the assumption that faithfulness lies primarily in orthodoxy.

Religious Educational Development

In addition to his work with the social forms within which education occurs, Moran has also elaborated a developmental perspective which, unlike many, honors the diversity, richness, and freedom of human development in faithfulness. His perspective contains a stage theory of growth in faithfulness, though he prefers to think in terms of "moments" rather than stages, and identifies this pattern as "religious educational development." According to Moran, these moments are the 1) Physical, 2) Visional/Mythical, 3) Narrative, 4) Systematic, 5) Journeying/Inquiry, and 6) Centering.

Unlike many contrived developmental systems, Moran's foray into developmental thinking succeeds in describing the real patterns of people's lives. It is also relatively free of abstraction. Moran's "moments" present a picture of human growth in which there is a prominent place for the "catechetical" or "confessional" function of religious education and for the promotion of theological competence and understanding. As such, the schema affirms the schooling function of which these are all expressions. Still, Moran's focus is unremittingly on a practice of religious education that serves the actual lives people lead and the concrete needs that emerge silently within people and in their intimate relations and social encounters. For example, in

speaking of the final—the "centering"—stage of older
adults' development, Moran concludes: "The final moment
of religious educational development includes waiting and
the help we can give, mainly by our presence, to those who
wait."[11] Few features of Moran's work reveal quite so well
the essential message of his thought: the need for active
members of the faith community to focus on what is real.
With the aging adult, especially the older, sick adult, we
promote the faithful life by waiting with and being present
to the member of the community who awaits death.

Moran has also called on religious educators to resist
the current fashion that divorces religious and moral life. He
is most critical of concepts of moral life that identify moral
development with the ability to articulate certain rational
principles of justice. Moran is strenuous in his objection to
the reduction of moral growth as the ability to "handle" the
rational puzzles of moral dilemmas. He is equally strong in
his objection to reducing morality to rational principles. In
contrast to some moral development theorists who focus on
rules and principles, Moran says: "Mature men and women
are governed by a discipline of life within a community that
shapes our character through visions, stories, rituals and
innumerable gifts." And, "We become moral people because
we share in the life of a moral community."[12] In his stron-
gest criticism of rationalistic approaches, one which makes
plain the priority Moran attaches to the everyday life, he
says: "Religious education should disassociate itself from
the snobbish arrogance of the moral development scheme
and start attending to the saints in our midst."[13]

GUSTAVO GUTIÉRREZ
AND THE THEOLOGICAL SHIFT

Gabriel Moran's view of the proper relationship between
education in all its dimensions and religious instruction or
schooling in religion bears a striking resemblance to Gustavo
Gutiérrez's discussion of the relationship between spiritual-

ity and theology. Both Gutiérrez and Moran insist that concrete, gracious, everyday Christian faithfulness is prior to
and to some extent in conflict with professional educational
or theological efforts to present a message and to explain the
meaning of faithfulness. They both have a sense that these
professional interventions, though helpful, essential, and
well-intentioned, nevertheless threaten the revelation of the
real which is available through contemplative being. We
turn then to Gutiérrez's thought.

The characteristic of Latin American liberation theology
that comes most readily to mind is advocacy of justice for
the poor. This theme is elaborated in at least four ways.
First, Latin American liberation theology is a perspective on
Christian life that focuses on the duty of Christians to
engage in struggles for justice for and with the poor. Second, the focus on justice for the poor requires social analysis and criticism of economic and political arrangements that
oppress them and brutalize their oppressors. Third, Latin
American liberation theology demands active solidarity with
the poor. Finally, engagement in conflict to overturn unjust
economic and social arrangements may be necessary to
authenticate this social solidarity in specific oppressive circumstances.

Though these features are truly definitive of Latin
American liberation theology, by themselves they fail to
reveal the depth of the meaning of this profound movement
of faithfulness. They also fail to note an even more basic and
revolutionary aspect of the message of liberation theology,
at least as articulated by Gustavo Gutiérrez, which is that
the call for active solidarity with the poor is a call to holiness, to faithfulness and joy even amidst terrible suffering
and martyrdom. And what is especially important for our
purposes in this book is Gutiérrez's insistence that the
power of the faithfulness being lived out among Latin American Christians is tied to establishing both the proper
sequence between spirituality and theology and the primacy
of spirituality.

As those privileged to have heard him lecture know, Gutiérrez, despite his great respect for and facility in academic theology, can be quite droll and ironic in responding to the smugness of academic theologians who ask, "What is the theology behind your spirituality?" For Gutiérrez, spirituality is a "way." The term "spirituality" cannot be used simply to mean the prayerful training of the inner self. Spirituality is a whole way, not only the life of prayer and inner discipline and purification. It is, Gutiérrez repeats with such jolting simplicity, "a way to follow Jesus Christ." This understanding of spirituality is "death to the alleged 'ways' that individualism of one kind or another create."[14]

Gutiérrez portrays the concreteness, everydayness, and specificity of spirituality—a way to be holy—in his exegesis of John 1:37-40. The text is:

> The two disciples heard him say this [John the Baptizer referring to Jesus as the Lamb of God], and they followed Jesus. Jesus turned, and saw them following, and said to them, "What do you seek?" And they said to him, "Rabbi" (which means Teacher), "where are you staying?" He said to them, "Come and see." They came and saw where he was staying; and they stayed with him that day, for it was about the tenth hour. One of the two who heard John speak, and followed him, was Andrew, Simon Peter's brother.

Now every aspect of the passage seems worthy of attention except that which is most ordinary and mundane, the apparently gratuitous reference to the "tenth hour," about 4 p.m. Yet Gutiérrez "milks" the moment a bit when exegeting the passage. He allows his hearers to become a bit puzzled by his interest in this irrelevant detail about the time of day when the two disciples encountered Jesus. Then he shows that a definitive feature of religious experience is revealed in the scriptural author's recollection and recording of the time of day of the encounter, "about the tenth hour." Gutiérrez's interpretation of why the time of the meeting is

included is that even many years later—John's Gospel being
the last written—the evangelist could not forget the time of
day, the precise hour of his encounter with the Lord. It is
emblazoned in memory, a clue to the power and vividness
of the experience. Gutiérrez uses this to show that a
"spirituality," a way to be holy, emerges from a situation at
a given time, with the utmost concreteness and specificity.
A way to be faithful emerges from historical experience,
"this" experience, here and now. This is the meaning, Gutiérrez tells us, of "drink[ing] from our own wells."[15] And
drinking from our own wells is also the meaning of "mindfulness."

This spirituality, this way to be faithful, flows from
silence, the silence of contemplation and the silence of
praxis, or action purified by contemplative silence. And theology, Gutiérrez tells us, follows spirituality; it is the second
moment, the moment of speech which comes after silence.[16]
Theology must serve spirituality; it must proclaim the vital
message that is rooted in experience, the experience of the
tenth hour, the experience of the extraordinary in the ordinary lives we live, the experience made possible in contemplation.

As I stated above, this relationship between spirituality
and theology is analogous to that between education and
schooling or instruction in religion as set forth by Moran.
First there is education, the complex pattern of relationships
that promote the truthful, nonviolent, receptive life, the
individual and communal response to life's joys and hopes,
suffering and pain. Schooling, whether it takes the form of
proclamation, catechesis, or theological study, is a second
moment. If this sequence is not honored, if, lacking humility or wisdom, we instruct and prescribe before we have lis-
tened to the rhythm of the common life, there is a very real
danger that orthodoxy will become a substitute for faithfulness. When this happens the lives of the people in the faith
community become both ethically and religiously impover-
ished.

JUDAISM AND THE FAITHFUL COMMUNITY

David Tracy has noted that liberation theology is in part, an effort to "re-Judaize" Christianity, to reestablish the priority of faithful human behavior.[17] Christians have much to learn about faithfulness from Judaism, but first a cautionary note must be struck. When Christians study Judaism and relations between Jews and Christians, it should never be purely instrumental in purpose. The reason for Christian dialogue with Jews and study of Judaism is not the perfection of Christianity. The conversation labeled "Theology of Jewish-Christian Relations" exists primarily to promote empathy and partnership and to encourage acknowledgement by Christians of responsibility—and in some cases guilt—for the long history of the "teaching of contempt" of Jews.

This said, it can then be acknowledged without slipping into a subtle supercessionism[18] that the communal vitality of Christianity is deeply enriched by encounter with the Judaism out of which it sprang, as well as with contemporary Jewish life. As Cardinal Joseph Bernadin has said, the alienation of Christianity from constructive links with Judaism "had the effect of deadening an important dimension of the Church's soul."[19] Bernadin's point is especially true of Christian efforts to promote faithfulness. These efforts, sometimes labeled "religious education," sometimes "pastoral ministry," can become routinized and function solely as instruments of institutional solidarity or a supposedly timeless orthodoxy. Jewish communal and educational values can be a "subversive memory," an antidote and a vitalizing influence.

A religious and cultural reality as complex and rich as biblical, historical, and contemporary Judaism is virtually impossible to encapsulate here. Still, four broad features of this rich heritage and continuing communal life can be identified and considered in light of our discussion of patterns of faithfulness and contemplative being. These elemental loyalties and values lie at the heart of religious Judaism, and they have much to say to Christians who are striving to build a truly faithful community. They are: 1) Judaism's focus on everyday life and its holiness; 2) the concern that education build up a sense of peoplehood and unity in the corporate life of Jews; 3) the conviction that awe and wonder define the faithful life, indeed that these qualities precede faith, in the sense of propositional or dogmatic belief; and 4) the insistence that religious knowledge be useful not only in construing the world but also in promoting moral life. Let us consider each of these values in turn.

Speaking of the Jewish attitude toward everyday life and its holiness, Rabbi Abraham Heschel says:

> The ineffable inhabits the magnificent and the common, the grandiose and the tiny facts of reality alike. Some people sense this quality at distant intervals in extraordinary events; others sense it in the ordinary events, in every fold, in every nook; day after day, hour after hour. To them things are bereft of triteness. Slight and simple as things may be—a piece of paper, a morsel of bread, a word, a sigh—they hide a never ending secret: a glimpse of God? Kinship with the Spirit of Being? An eternal flash of the will?[20]

Related to this sense of emergent grace in every moment of life is a conviction that religious life and righteousness entail a deep, abiding loyalty to one's own people and the unity of that people. The gracious encounter with God and meaning occurs in the everyday life of the community. As Martin Buber expressed the point:

> We expect a theophany of which we know nothing but the place and the place is called community. In . . . this expectation there is no single God's word which can be clearly known and advocated. But the words delivered are clarified for us in our own human situation of being turned to one another. There is no obedience to the coming one without loyalty to his creatures. To have experienced this is our way.[21]

Filled with a sense of the divine encountered in everyday life within the community, the Jew is a person alive with awe and wonder and gratitude. For Heschel this attitude precedes faith and is its indispensable foundation: "Awe precedes faith, it is at the root of faith. We must grow in awe in order to reach faith. Awe rather than faith is the cardinal attitude of the religious Jew."[22]

Finally, there is in Judaism a profound acknowledgment that compassionate, ethical behavior is superior to right religious knowledge—to orthodoxy—and that religious belief exists to promote the moral life. As Rabbi Marc Angel has said, "Judaism has been relatively unconcerned with dogma. . . . The overwhelming emphasis of Judaism has been on behavior."[23] This is not to say that religious knowledge is not viewed with profound respect in Judaism, for it is. Indeed, the sages say that an ignorant person cannot be a devout person. Citing the Talmud, Judaica scholar Jack Spiro says that study is deemed of such importance "that children in school may not be interrupted even for the rebuilding of the Temple."[24] But, Spiro continues, "we are repeatedly told in rabbinic literature, that knowledge is not an end in itself; it must lead to a higher purpose. He who has knowledge of the Torah but not fear of God is like the keeper of a treasury who has the inner key but not the outer key; he cannot enter."[25] The fear of God of which Spiro speaks expresses itself in worship and in abiding commitment to moral life. But worship can never be substituted for justice. As Heschel says, the essence of the prophetic message is that "man may not drown the cries of the oppressed with the sound of hymns."[26]

Just as Moran upholds the priority of education, understood as a life-long process of relationships, and Gutiérrez insists that spirituality precedes theology, the spirit of Judaism serves as a vivid reminder that all our efforts to build a faithful community rest on promoting an attitude of reverence for every aspect of everyday life. As we have seen, this vivid appreciation for the gifts of ordinary life is the fruit of a discipline of practice that focuses the members of the faith community on the present moment in a way free of irritation

and dispersion and therefore conscious of all the simple gifts
that prompt gratitude.

EDUCATION, CULTURE, AND THE CHURCH

Education can induce loyalty to the ultimate or it can, as
George Leonard observed, "turn a torrent into a trickle,"[27]
reducing human creativity and promoting only second-hand
knowledge, dead tradition, and unreflective behavior. Cultural influences also can either promote or retard the formation of contemplative being and therefore of faithfulness.
Finally, the church itself can play a positive or negative role,
advancing or retarding the formation of a faithful community. We turn, then, to a brief consideration of each.

Education, like culture and the church, is a complex
phenomenon. Education within the church is no less so.
There are many ways of explaining this complexity; one
clear analysis is that of Paul Tillich. In the essay "Theology
of Education," Tillich notes that education within the church
has three equally important and definitive purposes. These
are: 1) the induction of persons into the religious group and
the promotion of loyalty to that group and its perspectives
and patterns of behavior; 2) the development of skills and
other competencies desired within the religious group; and
3) freedom to grow into the full capacity of one's humanity
as understood within the religious group.[28] These purposes
can be labeled socialization, skill development, and education for human freedom. They are interconnected and each
aspect converges, ideally, in educational efforts to form a
contemplative and therefore faithful people. To be contemplative is the ultimate expression of freedom. In Christianity
we might say the contemplative being is one who gently but
persistently resists the Seven Deadly Sins. This resistance
becomes habitual—that is to say, the skill is developed—if
the Christian participates in the life of a socializing community which is itself a contemplative community. (In chapter
4, Gabriel Moran's identification of such a religious community as a "zone of silence" will be discussed).

It is easy enough to see how inordinate focus on any one feature of what Tillich names "church education," can limit the possibility of integrated educational formation. Mary Boys, in the excellent typology she develops in her book, *Educating in Faith*, shows how religious education in the United States has expressed itself in very different ways in response to placing a higher value on one or another of these purposes. Thus, "evangelism," some forms of "Christian education," and "Catholic education—catechesis" are historical expressions of an emphasis on socialization and the development of religious "skills," such as prescribed worship and orthodox belief. The religious education movement, beginning early in this century and expressing itself in many ways in our time, lays the emphasis on human development or freedom.[29]

Boys' own constructive and original definition of religious education as "the making accessible of the traditions of the religious community and the making manifest of the intrinsic connection between traditions and transformation"[30] also reveals the complexity of education and the ease with which imbalance can occur. Boys' formulation is conceptually elegant and has in fact inspired enhanced practice, but it is relatively easy to see how tradition might be handled in a less than creative way, or transformation might give rise to trendiness in educational efforts to form a faithful people.

The cultural context, as well, makes it difficult to form a contemplative people. The general culture does not support being contemplative, nor does it encourage professionals within the faith community to make the formation of contemplative people their highest goal. Consumerism, individualism, and mobility promote a general situation of what Zen master Nhat Hanh calls "scatteredness" or "dispersion." The difficulties are clear.

Despite these negative forces, professional religious educators and pastoral ministers within the church in the United States have actually made great strides in practice which is both sensitive to the patterns and needs of people's ordinary lives and, at least implicitly, concerned about their interior lives. Still, the professional culture of control and the broader culture, with its centrifugal pull and resulting scatteredness, often diminish the ability of even these alert and well-intentioned people to promote contemplation. Programs and messages are always threatening to gain ascendence. And the professional imagination, for all the talk of "spirituality," has not yet fully grasped what it means to help nurture true silence and form mindful, peaceful people through a steady and sustained initiative within local religious communities.

Henri Giroux provides an analysis that helps to explain both the culture of control and the way it undermines contemplative formation. He sees the predominant ideology of our culture flowing from the influence of "technocratic rationality." In *Ideology, Culture and the Process of Schooling*, Giroux says that technocratic rationality "takes as its guiding interest the element of control, prediction, and certainty." This he contrasts with "interpretive rationality," which

> has a deep-seated interest in understanding the communicative and symbolic patterns of interaction that shape individuals and subjective meaning rather than focusing on or taking for granted the *a priori* forms of knowledge; its constitutive interest lies in understanding how the forms, categories and assumptions beneath the texture of everyday life contribute to our understanding of each other and the world around us.[31]

Giroux's idea corresponds with Moran's notion that religious educators must be respectful as well as "participating observers" of the lives of those whom they would serve; it is consistent with Gutiérrez's insistence that a way of life, a "spirituality," precedes theological formulation, and with the Jewish value of sanctifying the events of everyday life. Though Giroux makes no reference to the link, his perspective on knowledge and sympathetic receptivity are remarkably similar to Zen Buddhist ideas about how true knowledge is had: through attentive awareness, moment by moment.

The educational work is complex and the general culture is not always or often conducive. And the church itself plays an ambiguous role in the formation of a contemplative people and of a faithful community. This is not the place for a full-blown ecclesiological analysis, but one fundamental point can be made: a fundamental conflict resides at the very heart of the reality of the church. This conflict can be expressed by pointing to the aspect of the church as "institution" or as "mystical communion,"[32] or as the dynamic of "charisma" and "routinization" in the life of the church.[33] It has given rise in the history of the church to forms as different as the "church" and the "sect,"[34] or the "triumphalist" church with its "integralist" goals and the "servant" church which shares the "joys and hopes" of all humanity.[35] This fundamental conflict also led the nineteenth-century Liberal Protestant biblical scholars and students of religionsgeschichte (history of religion) to insist that only the reign of God in people's hearts mattered; the form and substance of the church in both orthodox Protestant and Catholic trappings was, for them, mostly extraneous if not positively destructive.[36] Tillich's distinction between the "church" and the "spiritual community"[37] and Karl Rahner's lament of the church's "boring administration" and "spiritual mediocrity"[38] both reflect this conflict at the very heart of the reality of the church, which is revealed when some continue to speak or act as if it were divided into two classes of people: the "church teaching" and the "church taught," while others insist upon the conciliar "People of God" vision and ideal. With these differing views of the church, it is not always clear what is the role or purpose of education in the church.

What is clear is that religious education as interpretive and sympathetic engagement with members of the gathered local church, day in and day out, taking its cues from the joys and sorrows of everyday life, with the end (purpose) of promoting a more faithful and truthful, receptive, and non-violent people, is not possible when the structures and the officials of a highly institutional church focus the resources and power of that institution on the preservation of linguistic and ritual orthodoxy and assent of the members to the truth of official dicta. It is also clear that a church dominated by institutional values will never embrace the priority of contemplative formation, for officials of such a church will, despite prevailing rhetoric, always be more interested in inducing uniform acquiescence to orthodox notions of creed, code, cult(us) and canon than nurturing contemplation and a truly prayerful and therefore prophetic people. In such an institutional environment those who work to build an authentically faithful community may actually be perceived as subversive.

It is ironic that the Catholic Church, for all the richness of authentic spirituality and communality it nurtures, is at the same time the expression of church life in which institutionalized values predominate, for the classical Catholic theological self-understanding—its doctrine of creation and grace and anthropology—is the basis for the freedom to prize and promote the disclosure of the Transcendent, which is the fruit of contemplation. Such freedom is expressed with beauty in Rahner's words about being itself: "anything is or has being in proportion to the degree in which it is subjectivity in possession of itself."[39] The priority of contemplative formation is enhanced by the true humanism and the radical doctrine of grace which is the Catholic birthright, what Rosemary Haughton has named "The Catholic Thing." It is helpful to examine this theological tradition in comparison with the Protestant spirit.

The Reform Protestant intuition, rooted in Pauline anthropology, is about the depth and pervasiveness of human brokenness, the fragmentation and distortion of the human spirit. But alongside this profound insight there is what Richard McBrien has called the original Thomistic intu-

ition about the divine-human encounter, "the presence of
God in the knowing subject . . . nature includes the radical
capacity for grace."[40]

The implications of this theological understanding and
its relationship to the themes of this chapter are made
clearer by the Protestant theologian Langdon Gilkey. His
assessment of the Catholic spirit is that:

> Catholicism has a continued experience unequaled in
> other forms of Western Christianity of the presence of
> God and of grace mediated through symbols to the entire
> course of *ordinary human life*, . . . of transcendent mystery
> impinging continually on human existence.[41]

The difference between a church dominated by institutional values and one which prizes contemplative formation
as a means of paying attention to and sanctifying elemental
human experiences, desires, relations, and social tasks is
expressed in Rosemary Haughton's distinction between two
forces struggling for the Christian soul: "Mother Church,"
and "Sophia":

> [Mother Church] . . . that domineering, occasionally
> smothering, always self-assured old lady . . . with her
> vast compassion and efficiency and her low estimate of
> human moral worth . . . [who practices] a lunatic tidiness
> that tries to legislate creation into some humanly control-
> lable pattern. . . . [And Sophia] . . . God active and orig-
> inal creating and teaching. Her job is a kind of cosmic
> home-making, creating from within rather than from
> without. . . . Wisdom [Sophia] is at home to callers and
> here . . . she gives splendid parties to which all are
> invited . . . assembled to celebrate the joy at the heart of
> reality in a thoroughly Catholic way with everyday food,
> with music and poetry, with ancient symbols and modern
> interpretations, with wordless awareness of the divine
> wisdom.[42]

What Haughton contrasts as "lunatic tidiness" and
"wordless awareness of the divine wisdom," Karl Rahner

speaks about in distinguishing "explanation" from the deeper experience and source of faithfulness: "letting oneself sink trustfully into the incomprehensible mystery":

> The act of accepting existence in trust and hope is therefore, if it does not misinterpret itself, the act of letting oneself sink trustfully into the incomprehensible mystery. Therefore, my Christianity, if it is not to misinterpret itself, is letting myself sink into incomprehensible mystery. It is therefore anything but an "explanation" of the world and my existence, [it is] much more an instruction not to regard any experience, any understanding (however good and illuminating they may be) as final, as intelligible in themselves.[43]

In his film *Star Wars*, Steven Spielberg places on Obi Wan's lips the words, "Use the force, Luke; let go. . . ." Meister Eckhart says that when we let go God begins to be. Nhat Hanh says that we stop and observe in order to arrive at liberation. Rahner enjoins us to "let ourselves sink into incomprehensible mystery." Many paths lead to the same conviction that the essence of a faithful life rests on formation in contemplative being. A truly faithful community is one in which such formation is given the highest priority. I have tried to show how educational and theological insights confirm this priority. I have also indicated some of the difficulties involved in achieving a state of affairs in which contemplation is, in fact, given this privileged place in the formative activities of the members of the faith community. Given these difficulties, it seems prudent to expand the analysis in the next chapter, showing how a number of influential thinkers identify the work of contemplative formation as an educational work. This further analysis will also entail recapping the essence of the experience called "contemplative being."

Chapter Three

"The Vocation to Be a Subject": Contemplative Formation and Religious Education

The quotation contained in the title of this chapter is from the writings of Paulo Freire, when he says that the goal of education is to assist persons in their "ontological vocation to be subjects."[1] Contemplative formation, like education, is also an assistance in becoming subjects. The link between the goals of contemplative formation and religious education is clear in remarks about teaching and learning in Zen Buddhist tradition from Sunyana Graef:

> A Zen master "teaches" in the same sense that a midwife "delivers" a baby. Neither could do the job lacking the fundamental elements. In the case of a midwife, it is the mother who bears the baby. In the case of a Zen teacher, it is the student who possesses what Buddhists call true nature: a mind of infinite depth and joy, compassion, wisdom, perfection, and lucidity. Everyone has this true nature or wisdom-mind as a birthright. Awakening, which is the experience of seeing this for oneself, is, for Zen, the truest form of learning.[2]

Socrates employed the same metaphor to describe his teaching: *maieutic*, or midwifery. And it reappears in the work of a modern feminist philosopher of education, May Field Belenky, who tells us that the "midwife teacher helps students deliver their words to the world."[3]

Many of the leading writers in religious education[4] implicitly or explicitly point out the urgency of adopting a mode of practicing religious education in the churches that delivers people to themselves, that awakens us, that helps form contemplatives. This chapter surveys some of the writings of some of these thinkers. But first, it will be helpful to focus on the mode of knowing, the attitudes and the experiences which constitute contemplative being. Then the link between the contemplative's gentle striving to make of life— moment by moment—an "inimitable masterpiece" and religious education's way of faithfulness will be seen more readily.

CONTEMPLATION AND KNOWLEDGE: HOW SHALL WE KNOW THE REAL?

The state of being of the contemplative person, as Thomas Merton tells us, is being fully awake, fully alive. This state is linked to engaging reality, to living *in* reality. Our guides in approaching some knowledge of the contemplative state are forthright in saying that being contemplative is being real, living in reality, even knowing the Real, or as Merton, says, vivid realization of the Source.

In Christian tradition, Saint Paul speaks of living *in* God when he quotes a religious saying of his day: "Yet [God] is not far from each one of us, for 'In God we live and move and have our being'"(Acts 17:27-28). In Taoist wisdom, Chuang Tsu speaks of being born and living in Tao, the Way:

> Fish are born in water
> Men are born in Tao
>
> If fish born in water seek the deep shadow
>   of pool and pond
> all their needs are satisfied
>
> If men born in Tao sink into the deep
>   shadow of non-action
> To forget aggression and concern
> They lack nothing
> Their lives are secure

Moral: All the fish needs is to get lost in the water
All men need is to get lost in Tao.[5]

Speech about the "Real" may seem to display ignorance of the central epistomological problem: how shall we know the Real? The meditative and contemplative traditions give an answer: knowing what is real, being real, living *in* the Real, is the fruit of immediacy; that is, it is the result of cultivating a certain awareness and deportment moment by moment. This being real and living *in* the Real—in Christian mysticism, life lived in the presence of God—is sharply distinguished from statements about what *is* real. In Taoism, the distinction is expressed in the saying of Lao Tsu in the *Tao Te Ching*, number 56, that those who say don't know; those who know don't say. In his *Pensees*, Pascal links wisdom to awareness of the immediacy of experience: "We recall the past; we anticipate the future as if we found it too slow in coming. . . . We are so unwise that we wander about in times that do not belong to us, and do not think of the only one that does."[6]

In *Seeds of Contemplation* the young monk Thomas Merton prays that he will be delivered from the whole burden of opinion he says he is not required to carry, as if objectified thinking and discourse would render his contemplative goal more remote. Heidegger asserts in *Being and Time* that human beings, anxiously yearning for authenticity and fullness of being, are thwarted by "chatter." And Polanyi's idea in *The Tacit Dimension* that such a tacit realm of knowledge exists in each of us, a realm of which we cannot speak, corresponds to the general contemplative insight that a truthful life and a knowledge of the Real does not lie at the end of the path of objectified rationality.

The contemplative person is one who has transcended the delusional thinking of ego-centeredness and its legacy of irritation, jealousy, anger, and anxiety. The contemplative person has somehow brought under control the forces of dispersion, scatteredness, and raggedness that accost us all.

Achieving this state over and over again, moment by moment, contemplative persons have opened to them a mode of knowing anchored in their presence to the immediacy of experience. Such persons, in Nhat Hanh's phrase, light "the torch of our awareness": "Let us light the torch of our awareness and learn again how to drink tea, eat, wash dishes, walk, sit, drive, and work in awareness. We do not have to be swept along by circumstances. We are not just a leaf or a log in a rushing river."[7]

In Zen, a preferred name for the knowledge that comes from this awareness or presence, this readiness each moment, is "mindfulness." The knowledge of mindfulness is like a flowing river, not like a block of content. The state of mindfulness is what Chuang Tsu calls "Great Knowledge":

> Great Knowledge sees all in one.
> Small knowledge breaks down into many.
> When the body sleeps, the soul is enfolded in One.
> When the body wakes, the openings begin to
>   function.
> They resound with every encounter,
> With all the varied business of life, the strivings
>   of the heart;
> Men are blocked, perplexed, lost in doubt.
> Little fears eat away their peace of heart.
> Great fears swallow them whole.
> Arrows shot at a target: hit and miss, right
>   and wrong.
> That is what men call judgement, decision.
> Their pronouncements are as final
> As treaties between emperors.
> O, they make their points! Their arguments fall
>   faster and feebler
> Than dead leaves in autumn and winter.
> Their talk flows out like piss,
> Never to be recovered.
> They stand at last, blocked, bound, and gagged,
> Choked up like old drain pipes.
> The mind fails. It shall not see light again.[8]

In contrast to the mind which is blocked and unreceptive to "Great Knowledge," there is the mind that practices mindfulness—awareness, a calm comportment, silence, receptivity, emptiness, and non-action—in the sense of acting with composure rather than in a dispersed, ragged, and scattered way.

The great pastoral theologian Joseph Jungmann said of catechesis that it must "furnish light for desire." It is the same for religious education focused on contemplative formation as the key to faithfulness. Religious education must encourage yearning for contemplative being, and it must show people how to practice to "crack the shell" (in Meister Eckhart's metaphor) of delusion, dis-ease, dispersion:

> The shell must be cracked apart if what is in it is to come out, for if you want the kernel you must break the shell and therefore, if you want to discover nature's nakedness you must destroy its symbols and the farther you get in the nearer you come to its essence. When you come to the One that gathers all things up into itself, there you must stay.[9]

CONTEMPLATIVE FORMATION AND RELIGIOUS EDUCATION

A remarkable range of writers treat qualities of contemplative being under titles like education, religious education, and faith development. Issues such as subjectivity, encounter with the Real, simplicity, awareness, presence, silence, and even emptiness are prominent in the thought of many influential authors in these fields. We begin a survey of some of these works with a consideration of subjectivity by one of the most influential of these thinkers, James Fowler.

Writing of the stage of faith that he designates "individuative-reflective faith" (a stage which corresponds in his system to healthy and mature adult religiousness for many), Fowler says:

> There must be a shift in the sense of the grounding and orientation of the self. From a definition of self derived

from one's relations and roles and the network of expectations that go with them, the self must now begin to be and to act from a new quality of self-authorization.[10]

Though the description may be interpreted as somewhat individualistic, a more sympathetic interpretation is that Fowler is depicting the healthy and mature religious adult as one who dwells in the realm of his or her subjectivity. Other features of Fowler's work make clear that this self-authorization is a springboard to genuine mutuality. In this his vision corresponds to that of the great meditative and contemplative traditions. Contemplative being is existence which derives its power and authenticity from contact with one's center, from dwelling in one's center, indeed dwelling in what Plotinus called "the center of centers." It is a mode of existence from which one reaches out in active love to others.

Similarly, in the work of religious educator John Westerhoff the goal of education is related to achieving subjectivity, this time expressed in terms of the metaphor of "heart." Writing of religious education in its particular function of "spiritual catechesis," Westerhoff says that such educational activity must help us "pay attention to the deep restlessness in our hearts," and in doing so achieve solitude and a "stewardship of time."[11]

And in a work that deserves to be broadly read and which is pivotal to any consideration of contemplation and religious education, Thomas Del Prete presents us with a comprehensive and compelling study of the explicit and implicit educational thought of Thomas Merton. In *Thomas Merton and the Education of the Whole Person*, Del Prete says that for Merton "learning is 'educational' when it is linked in some way to the process of *realizing our selves more deeply as persons* through the love of God."[12]

Merton, we are told, linked this kind of education to the virtue of simplicity. He was much taken with Saint Bernard's notion of God's gift of "natural simplicity"; Del Prete tells us that for Merton "this natural simplicity is an inherent quality of our being, an expression of the unity of our own being and life."[13] (This is also an important theme for Westerhoff, who says that "inner simplicity results is an outward simplicity of life style. Unless we experience the inward reality of letting go of our need to control, we cannot be freed to live simply."[14])

For Merton, simplicity is also linked to sincerity, a virtue he saw exemplified in a special way in Mark Van Doren, his teacher at Columbia University. Sincerity is a means of openness to our own subjectivity as well as to reality itself:

> "Sincerity is fidelity to the truth," Merton writes. Our truthfulness, in faithfulness "to ourselves, to God and to the reality around us," makes us sincere, makes us more authentically and fully ourselves. . . . Merton values van Doren's sincerity precisely for the humble fidelity to truth that it demonstrated. With his "clear mind" Van Doren "looked directly at the quiddity of things," their essential nature.[15]

Each of these authors shares the contemplative value of realizing the self, of shifting the ground of the self from superficial and unauthentic consciousness and action to a kind of truthfulness. Also common to both educational and contemplative language is the idea that each is delivery of the self to the Real. For example, Parker Palmer, speaking of contemplative education—what he calls "education in [and centered on] transcendence"—says that it

> prepares us to see beyond appearances into the hidden realities of life—beyond facts into truth, beyond self-interest into compassion, beyond our flagging energies and nagging despairs into the love required to renew the community of creation.[16]

And Fowler speaks in a similar vein when he points to a time in life in which the issue of "partnership with the Transcendent" becomes urgent: "Having found the limits of self-groundedness as the basis for our lives, strangely we are open in new ways to falling in love with the true Ground of our Being."[17]

Another distinguished religious educator, once again employing language which is common in the literature of contemplation, speaks of retrieval of subjectivity and delivery to the Real. In his discussion of prayer in *Vision and Character*, Craig Dykstra links prayer to paying attention: "the discipline of paying attention to what God has given us . . . [which] start[s] by learning to pay attention . . . to the reality before us . . . takes us out of ourselves and then changes us to bring us more in accord with reality."[18] Dykstra's treatment of paying attention calls to mind the Western notion of the practice of the presence of God and the Zen Buddhist idea of the centrality of awareness which is both cause and effect of concentration (*samadhi*) and understanding (*prajna*).

These authors, consistent with the meditative and contemplative traditions, reject the idea that objective knowledge is the ultimate source of meaning or the primary goal of education. Palmer says, "Objectivism tells the world what it is rather than listening to what it says about itself. . . . [Objectivism is] a way of knowing that places us in an adversary relation with the world.[19] And James Fowler, writing of highly mature "conjunctive" religious faith, identifies its presence in part with the ability of the human spirit to know in a paradoxical way—what the mystic Nicholas of Cusa called "the coincidence of opposites" and C. G. Jung changed to the "conjunction of opposites." This paradoxical knowing, which is the antithesis of objective knowing, "gives rise to second naivete, a post-critical receptivity," with which Fowler identifies deeply developed spiritual life and which is certainly only available in contemplative practice.[20]

Finally, Del Prete evokes Merton's view of education, writing:

> If it is to nurture the growth of the true self, education will clearly have to nourish a subjective experience of knowing. Education driven solely by a view of knowledge as a matter of discrete and objective, if not manipulable, entity

will provide little support for self-discovery. Such education habitually removes knowledge from the realm of personal experience and connectedness to the world. It fails to enhance one's sense of reality and is thus lifeless."[21]

In most traditions of mysticism, meditation, and contemplation, the emphasis is on practice: contemplative being is not achieved at the end of a path strewn with speculation but is the continuing outcome of meditative or contemplative practice. This is what is behind the saying of the Zen master Shunryu Suzuki, "How to sit is how to act."[22] The practice of *Zazen*—seated meditation in Zen Buddhism—is meant to serve as a model for every other act throughout the day, each day of a person's life; "in activity calmness, in calmness activity."[23]

If we take "mindfulness" as the single most adequate designation of the psychological state of a contemplative person, we again see that the religious educators whose thought we are surveying point to an ideal of formation in faithfulness which is equivalent to contemplative formation. We have seen that mindfulness expresses itself functionally in presence: a steady, disciplined ability to actually inhabit the present time. No such "presence to the present" is possible without cultivating disciplines of emptying, emptying the mind of distractions which cause irritation, frustration, dispersion or scatteredness, anger, envy, jealousy, and the anxiety of being tied to the past or pulled into the future. We have also noted that the emptiness of the mind, its capacity to concentrate (*samadhi*) requires the practice of silence.

Against this background, consider Westerhoff's idea, to which passing reference was made earlier, that a goal of "spiritual catechesis" is to assist people to practice "stewardship of time": "Just thinking about all we have to do exhausts us. Time has us, we do not have time. . . . The contemplative life provides us with the redemption of time."[24] Westerhoff also speaks of silence as the condition for presence, linking it to stewardship of time and the ability to overcome busyness: "when we can embrace solitude and silence. . .we become aware that our worth is not the same as our usefulness."[25]

Del Prete, using Merton's own experience and values as a model of the "education of the whole person," says of him:

His voice emerged from silence and testified to what in silence was revealed as real, to life. In silence resounded an innocence and authenticity beyond his own predilection, his own thought, his own prejudice and that of his society; thus silence attuned him to understand on a level of existential reality and nurtured authenticity in his own voice. To speak authentically from silence, therefore, required a vigilant openness and disinterest, in effect the same attentive process of learning to see, hear, speak and discern inherent to the formation of the whole person.[26]

In language remarkably similar to that employed by Zen Buddhism to designate the goal of Zen, James Fowler speaks of the final state of faithfulness as a state of emptiness, *shunyata* in Sanskrit. In this state, silence having rendered the person utterly present to or aware of reality in all its simplicity as it unfolds moment by moment, there is no "place" in a person's inner self for "foreign objects" such as irritation, frustration, dispersion or scatteredness, anger, envy, jealousy, and anxiety caused by being pulled into the future. This "place" is empty, able to receive and to be awake. We have achieved "poverty" in the sense Meister Eckhart employs the term. This mindfulness, or emptiness or poverty, is also called concentration. So great is the importance attached to this simple, elemental state of mind and heart that Shunryu Suzuki says that to be concentrated on nothing is freedom itself.

For Fowler, emptiness is the state of "Universalizing faith," "a transformed and transforming relationship to the ultimate conditions of life." Fowler describes Universalizing faith in these words:

The person [of] Universalizing faith has assented to a radical decentrating from the self . . . and has begun to manifest the fruits of a powerful kind of *kenosis* or emptying of self. Often described as "detachment" or "disinterested-ness," the *kenosis*—literally, the "pouring out" or empty-ing of self . . . is actually the fruit of having one's affections powerfully drawn beyond the finite centers of value and power that promise meaning and security.[27]

In each of these authors there is a remarkable corre-spondence between the values and attitudes which are ascribed to education in faithfulness and the purposes of meditation and contemplation. Each is preoccupied with subjectivity, with paying attention and therefore discovering the real in the immediacy of experience, with simplicity, silence, presence, and emptiness. We now turn to two other authors to extend this analysis and confirm the intimate rela-tionship between our educational efforts to build a faithful community and the formation of contemplative people.

THE RELIGIOUS EDUCATORS OF CONTEMPLATIVE FORMATION

The works of two theorists writing in the field of religious education express in an explicit way the relationship between education and contemplation. For one, Maria Harris, contem-plation is the model for teaching and learning. For the other, Gabriel Moran, contemplative being is the end or purpose of religious education and of the life of the religious community.

Maria Harris

In speaking of the relationship between students and teach-ers, Maria Harris describes four features which should pre-dominate. Student and teachers are *sacraments* to one another; they are *co-creators*, whose relationship is marked by *asceticism*, a repudiation of manipulation. But first of all, Harris tells us, student and teacher are *co-contemplatives*. Clearly, for Harris contemplative formation ranks high in the aims of religious education.[28] Even when she is dealing with educational macro-planning for the whole religious

community, as in *Fashion Me a People*, Harris calls for a dis-
position of contemplation as a necessary foundation. One of
the best sources for a picture of the importance Harris places
on contemplative being in teaching and learning is the quite
remarkable chapter of *Teaching and Religious Imagination* in
which she examines teaching itself.[29]

Harris begins her appraisal of teaching as a contemplative activity by rejecting two other models of teaching. The
first is the idea that teaching is best understood as a matter
of technique. (This is a criticism that brings to mind Parker
Palmer's rejection of curiosity by itself as an adequate basis
for knowing and for humane education.[30]) The second
model of teaching that Harris rejects is the identification of
teaching with "mastery of content." (Again there is a corre-
spondence with Palmer's thought; he also rejects control as
the primary motive for knowing, insisting that compassion
is a more adequate basis than curiosity or control.) Harris
believes that an alternate basis for conceiving the act of
teaching is to "bring to it an attitude similar to that which
we bring to any work of art," and that is the attitude of
receptivity. With this starting point, Harris establishes her
model as a contemplative one.

Harris then names and explains five moments or steps
(in the sense of dance steps) that define the act of teaching:
contemplation, engagement, form-giving, emergence, and
release. My own assessment of her analysis is that, taken
together, all five steps constitute a deeply resolute and sustained activity of contemplation.

CONTEMPLATION

Regarding the first step, Harris says that good teaching is
steadfastly—but gently and graciously—attentive to what is
there; it begins in stillness, an attitude of silence and reverence. She refers to this as a kind of poverty, like the poverty
of *Shunyata* (emptiness), or, as noted above, the poverty to
which Meister Eckhart refers when, speaking of the mystical
experience, he says: "It is here in this poverty that man

regains the eternal being that once he was, now is and ever more shall be."[31]

With this poverty there is simplicity, the intellectual simplicity that comes from natural simplicity, to which Saint Bernard refers. Harris cites Annie Dillard's story of the person with such "healthy poverty and simplicity . . . that finding a penny will literally make [her] day," and concludes that these characteristics are the "necessary conditions for hope, for possibility, for the future."

ENGAGEMENT

Engagement for Harris is "diving in, wrestling with and rolling around in subject matter." This is not itself the stuff of contemplation but, as her subsequent analysis makes clear, such engagement is possible only when the teacher is contemplative. Harris links engagement and contemplation when she notes that the first resistance to engagement is "dilettantism," a superficial approach to the subject matter which she contrasts with love of the subject matter. Harris, like Thomas Merton, also invokes Mark Van Doren, the teacher Merton so admired for his simplicity, his sincerity, his commitment to the "quiddity" of reality. Harris also sees Van Doren as exemplar of the contemplative teacher, one whose engagement with subject matter and with "subjects who matter" possesses all these contemplative characteristics.

The second resistance to teaching as engagement also reveals the need for a contemplative spirit; it is the "fear of our own creativity." This resistance is overcome when teachers experience that "our own creativity is not the only creativity operating." Here Harris speaks of deliverance from fear, from restraint, from a kind of timidity that we shake loose of when we experience the presence of the Reality apprehended in contemplation. The ability to become engaged, to dive in, wrestle and roll, is an experience of liberation. Harris' discussion of resistance to engagement brings to mind Meister Eckhart's, "There where clinging to things ends, God begins to be born,"[32] or Thomas Merton's famous essay, "The General Dance," in which "we are invited to forget ourselves on purpose, cast our awful solemnity to the winds and join in the general dance."[33]

The final resistance to teacher engagement is "the misunderstanding of what it is to be an artist," for the teacher is an artist. "We misunderstand what it is to be a teacher," Harris tells us, ". . . if we think that teaching simply means to hand on, hand over or convey subject matter merely as a system of clues." This reductionist understanding corresponds to our earlier discussion of objectivism.

In contrast to the teacher as one who hands on clues, Harris' teacher is a contemplative helping to nurture contemplatives, whose words resemble those of Zen teachers such as Sunyana Graef, whose thoughts about contemplative education are like those of the Western and Eastern mystics who discuss subjectivity and its relationship to the Real. Like Graef, Harris says, "Teaching is the creation of a situation in which subjects, human subjects, are handed over to *themselves.*" Like Merton speaking of the knowledge of the Source, Harris tells us that when teaching as engagement delivers persons to their subjectivity it is delivering them to the Real, delivering them to

> the Subjectivity of subjectivity: the belief that everything and everyone in existence draws that existence from participation in the One Who Is, and that any human subjectivity which exists does so by reason of its own being in, dwelling in and having been created in the fullness, richness and depth of the Subjectivity of God.

FORM-GIVING

In her discussion of form-giving, the third step in the teaching act, Harris turns her attention again to subject matter and how it can be understood either as a system of "clues" or a "labyrinth of reality," or as content. She also addresses form-giving as formation and information. The contemplative element of this step is revealed in Harris' discussion of three features of teaching as form-giving: 1) teacher intentionality; 2) the forms that ground our engagement in formation and information; and 3) the risk contemplative teachers must take in order to accept their identity as artists.

Those familiar with Maria Harris' work know of her commitment to knowledge, to erudition as an integral feature of education, whether in or out of schools. But Harris, like Goethe, would certainly consider the merely well-informed person the most useless bore on the face of the earth. Still, her commitment to traditional instructional goals is clear. Against this background, Harris' challenge to the teacher as form-giver is startling, for she says that "for true form-giving to occur any and all prior *absolute conviction* regarding the *exact* nature of the form itself must be absent" (emphasis mine).

This means that good teaching, teaching that emerges from a contemplative center, rests on a willingness to allow content to emerge, discourse to occur, and ideas and insights to develop which were not necessarily precisely what the teacher intended, perhaps not at all what the teacher intended. Even a teacher like Harris, who respects inherited knowledge, has a commitment to erudition, and decries cultural, historical, and ideational illiteracy hiding behind appeals to experience, must possess the discipline and humility to suspend *absolute* conviction about the *exact* nature of what should be learned in a particular moment if education is truly to occur. Harris quotes John Dewey saying, "Perhaps the greatest of all pedagogical fallacies is that people learn the thing they are studying at the time they are studying it." Harris' insight about teacher willingness to let go of absolute intentionality rests on her own humanistic impulses as well as on a philosophy of knowing that resembles that of Zen Buddhism. Consider these words of Nhat Hanh:

> Thinking is to take cinder blocks of concepts from the memory warehouse and build monuments. We call these hovels and palaces "thoughts." But such thinking, by itself, has no creative value. It is only when lit by understanding that thinking takes on real substance. Under-

standing does not arise as a result of thinking. *It is the result of a long process of conscious awareness.*[34]

This kind of discipline, this kind of professional and intellectual *kenosis*—as the discussion of objectivism earlier in this chapter suggests—is the fruit of the contemplative way of being. As we have seen, it is from the meditative and contemplative traditions of thought and practice that the suspicion of "absolute convictions" and the "exact nature" of content comes. It is only in these traditions of meditation and contemplation that continuous awareness is seen as the real source of insight. Only teachers who are contemplatively grounded are able to resist role expectations to promote evasive knowledge, the objectivism that both Harris and Palmer criticize. Liberated teachers are not unappreciative of the goals of cultural and historical literacy in educational practice. But the contemplative spirit allows them to alternate between these intentions and being awake to possibilities, to forms emerging in the immediacy of teacher and student awareness.

The ideal of the contemplatively grounded teacher as one who is able to nurture form is rounded out in Harris' discussion of the forms with which such teachers deal, or better perhaps, the forms which teachers and students encounter. Harris tells us that the "forms are not our ideas, our concepts, our learning. They are instead the grounds of those ideas, the roots of learning and the foundations of our lives: love, identity, death, intention, destiny, courage and hope."

Here we are surely confronted with the greatest challenge of all. How is a teacher who is committed to specific and identifiable intentions and instructional objectives nevertheless able to provide an environment in which others are alert to the ground of life itself? Harris believes that every occasion of engagement in education between teacher and student, regardless of the context or the "subject matter," is a potential occasion for encountering the ground, the roots, the depth of our lives—the Source of Reality. But no such possibility exists apart from contemplative practice and contemplative being. To serve both instructional goals and the more profound possibility of encountering elemental forms of human life, the teacher must practice what Eastern mystical tradition calls "non-doing" or "non-action."

The idea of non-doing or non-action and its practice are contained in a stanza from a saying of Chuang Tsu cited earlier in this chapter: "If men born in Tao sink into the deep shadow of non-action, to forget aggression and concern, they lack nothing, their lives are secure." In Chinese the ideal of non-action is expressed in the phrase *wei wu wei*, literally, "non-doing doing"; in Sanskrit the expression *anabhoga carya*, "non-clinging doing," captures the same state of being and ideal of practice. These are not slogans for withdrawal; they are appeals to cultivate as far as possible a mode of practice which, while set on its own course, is nevertheless alert and alive to insights that emerge from immediate awareness. So, while we do what we intend to do with great zeal, passion, and enthusiasm, our "doing" has about it a quality of grace, a willingness to be replaced by some greater revelation than that contained in our conscious intention. Thus, we call this doing "non-doing," this action "non-action."

To summarize in Western terms, Harris' third step in teaching challenges teachers to a discipline of form-giving as formation in contemplation, to a letting go of "absolute convictions" and the "exact nature" of the form. Harris challenges teachers to practice receptivity to the elemental forms that root and ground their conscious intentions; thus, she is calling teachers to contemplation.

EMERGENCE AND RELEASE

Harris' fourth and fifth steps in teaching, emergence and release, are readily identified as qualities of the meditative, contemplative person. For educated learning to emerge, one must cultivate a sensitivity to time, what Westerhoff calls "stewardship of time," and this requires patience. In her discussion of the need for patience in the step of emergence in teaching, Harris recalls the story in *Zorba the Greek* in which Zorba tells of destroying a chrysalis and the nascent butterfly within because of impatience. Donald Grey has also written eloquently of this quality of patience:

> Patience points us toward the given in human life. Patience compels us to perceive ourselves as receivers. From patience gratitude is born, for in the final analysis "what have you that you have not received?" (1 Cor. 4:7). . . . It is . . . possible for patience to enlarge the parameters of our receiving. Patience in this sense is openness, receptivity and vulnerability. . . . [it] is the antithesis of closemindedness, dogmatism and rigidity.[35]

In speaking of the fifth step, release, Harris comes full circle, explicitly invoking traditions of meditation and contemplation, the emptiness of the Zen *satori* experience, the receptivity and peace of the experience of sabbath. This culminating moment for the contemplative teacher is a possibility of holiness, "the holiness of the moment of release." Release, in the sense of delivering subjects to themselves and in the sense of the mystic's letting go, is, after all, the common purpose of teaching and contemplation.

Gabriel Moran

For Gabriel Moran, the promotion of contemplation—"an attitude of peace, wholeness, and centeredness"—is clearly the aim of religious education. But "the question is whether religious educators themselves see contemplation as a practical concern at the heart of religious education."[36] Moran suffers from no such ambiguity; for him both religion and education culminate in contemplation.

Moran believes the end or goal of religious development is the "parabolic attitude," a state of being in which the limits of objectified knowledge are clearly faced: "the parabolic attitude is the recognition that the search for answers must go on but with a different expectation of success. We realize that we are never going to reduce life to a rational system."[37]

The religious journey, as Moran sketches it, is precisely the contemplative journey: silence transforms awareness so that we let go of superficial and objectified aims and truth claims. We can then achieve a functional vision of the unity of reality—with its promise of compassion rooted in contemplation—and conquer corrosive preoccupation with allusions of the past or future by paying attention to the reality present in the immediacy of the experience of the silent self. Moran says of the religious journey:

> As imagination expands and the mind is quieted, we come to see the similarities among all things. Simultaneously we become detached from superficial perceptions of the self and from the apotheosis of any object. The journey to the One beyond all names is a trip of no further distance than a coming to awareness of oneself. . . . The formulas in religion are paradoxes that push our awareness back to the particular realities of everyday life. . . . Religious progress comes about by an increasing awareness of the interconnectedness of things. Imagination becomes less inadequate as we care deeply for things in their concreteness, their "suchness."[38]

All of the values in the language of contemplative being are here: silence, the identity of all existence, detachment without ceasing to be active and ask questions, the journey within (which is not an exercise in privatism), the encounter with life's "suchness," or quiddity. Because of Moran's belief in the convergent natures of religion and education, for him contemplative being is the end, or purpose, not only of religion but of education as well. The fully educated person is at leisure, "the stage [of educational development] at which we situate a fully developed self in a calmly accepted cosmos."[39]

There is more evidence in Moran's work that the goals of religious education and of contemplative formation are identical. As in the traditions of meditation and contemplation, in Moran's work the end of religious education is to be *awake*, and Moran's name for the free, healthy, centered person is the *mindful* person, the person who is *present*. For both Moran and the Eastern and Western mystical writers, a special form of *non-action* is to be cultivated. And for both, true *compassion* arises from the contemplative center of a person whose inner life has transcended preoccupation with trivialities and with a highly calculating, precisely rational understanding of good and evil.

The stories of the Buddha contain his own striking explanation of who or what he is, what he has experienced. As noted in chapter 1, in response to questions about his nature we are told that Shakyamuni Buddha explained that he is simply "awake." D. T. Suzuki speaks of this state as that brought about when Zen practice opens the "third eye," insight into our true being.[40] For Moran as well, awakeness is the end of religious development: "Religious development in the East seems mainly directed by the image of enlightenment. Western religion has leaned toward the image of revelation. . . . They agree upon the need to reach a true self by penetrating beyond a false self."[41]

Like Merton when he speaks of every event and moment sowing seeds and Nhat Hanh when he speaks of the moment as a miracle, Moran believes that the pinnacle of human development is a state of mindful, peacefully concentrated presence. Just as D. T. Suzuki warns that only dread lies in wait for the person who cannot convert "was" and "will be" to "is" and Nhat Hanh cautions that being pulled into the future renders a human being incapable of living even a single moment of their existence, Moran associates the scattered or dispersed life with loss of presence: "The future . . . can become an obsession which distracts humans from the present."[42] He writes:

> Where is the substance to any life if the past is no longer with us, the future has not arrived and the present is a fleeting moment. . . . The opposite of present is neither past nor future; the opposite of present is *absent*. I deny that one can overemphasize the present; the present is all there is and all there ever will be.[43]

Like authors who write explicitly of contemplative life, Moran associates mindfulness with non-action, the *wei wu wei* (non-doing doing) of the "true man of Tao." Agreeing with Keynes' criticism of the "sickness of purposefulness," Moran says, "The detached person may be active, but the word action has been transformed. One must act without looking for the 'fruit of one's action.' "[44]

The most crucial issue in the literature of contemplation and religious education, as I have tried to show, is the link between contemplation and compassion. Here again, Moran's contribution is substantial and the correspondence with contemplative language striking. Like the literature of meditation and contemplation, Moran's work points to the intimacy of the relationship between the mystical and the moral.

Just as Meister Eckhart links contemplation and love and Taisen Deshimaru does the same with the image of the Zen monk who will jump into hell for another, meditative enlightenment having made him that compassionate, Moran says "an educational morality must include an element of the mystical":

> To be morally adult is to know that the world does not divide into good and bad things, right and wrong choices. . . . If we let the choice flow from the *center of our receptivity to being* and in resonance with fellow travelers on earth, our actions will have a gentleness that lessens the violence in the world.[45]

Moran rejects the dichotomies between inner and outer, mystical and moral, contemplative and conscientious. Just as Merton dismisses the insidious association of contemplatives with naturally phlegmatic people who like to sit about, Moran says:

> Mystics are accused of fleeing the world and not facing reality. But . . . the truth is that the mystics not only "face reality" but embrace it, or rather are embraced by it. What is fled from is the trivializing attitude of grasping at goods

that the human cannot carry beyond death, or demanding rights to the exclusion of other creatures. The moral and mystical journey is not to ideal and spiritual forms above the world but to the deepest, darkest center of the material cosmos where goodness bubbles up in gentle, just and caring attitudes.[46]

For Moran, contemplative being and the compassionate response that is the heart of holiness is the major function of religious education; thus, contemplation is the key to forming faithful people and faithful communities. Indeed, for Moran the faithful community is quite simply a contemplative community. It is a community of presence, of silence and emptiness, of compassionate action emerging from the center:

> The words presence and community [are] synonymous: to be in a community is to be present. Presence is a mode of relationship which a person has to other persons, to oneself and to the world of non-persons. The greater the communal experience, the greater is the presence. . . . A religious community is a group whose rituals and symbols heighten presence.[47]

> Religious silence is . . . in the deeper life of the community: speech arises constantly from the well of silence and when one is finally speechless in ecstasy or sorrow, a silence that is full is at the center of things.[48]

> . . . a religious body [community] would have to provide for ego loss, that is, for a person going out of his or her mind without being destroyed. . . . [Silence, presence, and the quieting of destructive self-absorption being accomplished within the contemplative community,] a religious body [community] would [then] be a place for contemplative prayer, rhythmically related to intense social action.[49]

Religious and educational development culminate in contemplative being, and the truly faithful community increasingly expresses this being in its corporate reality, as each and every member of the community become progressively more contemplative, set upon living a truthful life: "a lifetime of patient attentiveness and nonviolent receptiveness."[50]

In a special way the religiously educating community—the community of contemplative formation—is the source from which we receive the strength to be contemplative at work and within the family. It is to contemplative attitudes about work and within the family that we turn in the next two chapters.

Chapter Four

"Washing the Dishes to Wash the Dishes": Work, Irony, and Contemplative Formation

Whether work functions in a person's life as "job," "career," or "calling" (to employ Robert Bellah's distinctions[1]), the emotional and material importance of work is self-evident. If work degenerates into drudgery, it has the potential to distort and destroy persons, relations, even cultures.

Aquinas said that there "can be no joy in life without joy in work."[2] Freud said that a sane person is one who is able to work as well as to love.[3] These two elements of sanity—work and love—are related. If one's work life entails unremitting competition and requires that one behave in purely expedient fashion, and if this work neither claims nor promotes one's loyalty to activity, excellence, or common effort, it is questionable whether "at the end of the work day" love is possible. As Dick Westley says: "The question becomes, is one who is present in a competitive way in the utilitarian world of work all day really able to be present in relational and expressive ways at home and at play?"[4]

Even the less dramatic situation, in which one's work life occupies what Peter Berger has called "a sort of grey, neutral region," reveals the relationship between spiritual well-being and work. Berger speaks of a "three-fold division of labor." First, there is "work that still provides an occasion for primary self-identification," an increasingly rare instance. Then there is "work apprehended as a direct threat to self-identification." Finally, in the most common circumstance, that which Berger speaks of as grey work, there "is work that is neither fulfillment nor oppression . . . in which one neither rejoices nor suffers, but with which one puts up with more or less grace for the sake of other things that are supposed to be important."[5]

It may be self-evident that oppressive work situations and even work in "grey regions" can have brutalizing effects. What is less obvious is that salvation of persons, relations, and cultures from starkly brutal work or, less dramatically, from the soul-sickness of limitation, frustration, and disappointment encountered in any work life, depends on a richly ironic humor and a comic spirit, for irony is an attitude which enables us to accept limitation without despair. Irony is the sense of proportion of which C. S. Lewis spoke, the absence of which he equated with Hell.[6] And comic humor, related to ironic humor, is the spirit's ability to soar despite the increasing constraints to which each of us is subjected as we take our places in the "real world," the "work world," the world in which we are encouraged to "behave like adults."

Work is an aspect of life in which a pervasive sense of limitation is experienced and expectations of restraint and "seriousness" are enforced. George Santayana could, I think, have been speaking of many people's work sites when he wrote: "Where the spirit of comedy has departed, company [or, The Company] becomes constraint, reserve eats up the spirit and people fall into a penurious melancholy in their scruple to be always exact, sane and reasonable." He adds, "Irony pursues these enemies of comedy."[7]

The contemplative way of being is a way of irony and of comedy. Mystical wisdom, whether it is framed in the language of Christian contemplation, or the way of Zen, or the life of awesome gratitude that Rabbi Heschel associates with the basic religious attitude, is an invitation gently to resist being swamped by irritation and anger caused in large measure by our work lives. The great sage of Taoism, Chuang

Tsu, addresses the relationship of work, irony, and contemplative calm in the story of "Three in the Morning":

> When we wear out our minds, stubbornly clinging to one partial view of things, refusing to see a deeper agreement between this and its complementary opposite, we have what is called "three in the morning."

> What is this "three in the morning?" A monkey trainer went to his monkeys and told them: "As regards your chestnuts: you are going to have three measures in the morning and four in the afternoon." At this they all became angry. So he said: "All right, in that case I will give you four in the morning and three in the afternoon." This time they were satisfied. The two arrangements were the same in that the number of chestnuts did not change. But in one case the animals were displeased, and in the other they were satisfied. The keeper had been willing to change his personal arrangement in order to meet objective needs. He lost nothing by it!

> The truly wise man, considering both sides of the question without partiality, sees them both in the light of Tao.[8]

Rabbi Heschel also addresses this relationship when he writes:

> He who wants to enter the holiness of the day must first lay down the profanity of clattering commerce, of being yoked to toil. He must go away from the screech of dissonant days, from the nervousness and fury of acquisitiveness and the betrayal in embezzling his own life. He must say farewell to manual work and learn to understand that the world has already been created."[9]

And the day whose holiness one would enter is not only the sabbath day. Ironic recognition that the world has already been created and the peaceful performance of our work that this recognition inspires is for the "workdays" as well: "The work on weekdays and the rest on the seventh day are correlated. The sabbath is the inspirer, the other days the inspired."[10]

To what else is the great Zen scholar, D. T. Suzuki, addressing himself but work, irony, and contemplative calm when he reports the *koan* or rationally inexplicable meditation problem common in some forms of Zen practice:

> Empty-handed I go and behold the
> spade is in my hand.
>
> I walk on foot and yet on the back of
> an ox I am riding.
>
> When I pass over the bridge
> Lo the water floweth not
> but the bridge doth flow.[11]

Similarly, we recognize the dis-ease, struggle, and turmoil of so many work sites and work lives in Katsuki Sekida's explicit statement about the relationship between contemplative calm and the healing of anger by laughter:

> Man is often surfeited with his own ego, with its antagonisms, its troubles, difficulties and internal strife. Consciously and unconsciously, he is seeking somewhere in the secret part of his mind a release from such burdens. When he encounters such relief in a smile or a laugh that cancels the world of opposition, he gives a sigh of relief and feels at rest. Each person's ego is like stockpiled atomic weapons; when a laugh disposes it, a peaceful world, comfortable to live in, is realized.[12]

Finally, from the Christian tradition, Jesus of Nazareth speaks of work, irony, and contemplative calm (and we must not miss the loving yet pointedly ironic flavor of the message) when he says:

> Therefore I tell you, do not be anxious about your life, what you shall eat or what you shall drink, nor about your body, what you shall put on. Is not life more than food, and the body more than clothing? Look at the birds of the air: they neither sow nor reap nor gather into barns, and yet your heavenly Father feeds them. Are you not of more value than they? . . . Consider the lilies of the field, how

they grow; they neither toil nor spin; yet I tell you, even Solomon in all his glory was not arrayed like one of these. But if God so clothes the grass of the field, which today is alive and tomorrow is thrown into the oven, will he not much more clothe you, O men of little faith? Therefore do not be anxious, saying, "What shall we eat?" or "What shall we drink?" or "What shall we wear?". . . . But seek first his kingdom and his righteousness, and all these things shall be yours as well. Therefore do not be anxious about tomorrow, for tomorrow will be anxious for itself. (Mt. 6: 25- 34)

WORK AS DRUDGERY

In *The Humanization of Man*, John Julian Ryan defined drudgery as "work performed in a spirit of boredom. . . . [the] distress of having to perform monotonously repetitive and uninteresting tasks without let up and unremittingly."[13] Under the influence of such drudgery, as well as the obsession with the profit motive, the human worker can be depicted as "essentially inartistic; naturally slothful [and] determinately individualistic."[14] But this is not how humans as workers are or are meant to be; we are only made so. Ryan cites Aristotle's statement that "pleasure naturally results from the strenuous use of one's powers; it is a by-product of normal intense functioning."[15] In what Ryan calls a "truly humane society," the person as worker would more regularly be able to take genuine pleasure in work; natural traits of artistry, activity, and cooperation would be allowed to flourish. He says: "man is primarily an artist, a person of technique. . . . [who] far from being sluggardly . . . is naturally active." As to narrowly individualistic and purely self-interested work, Ryan concludes:

> . . . it is absurd to imagine that man as a producer originally thought of himself as primarily concerned with his own individual gain. As a member of a family and a tribe, he would never have known what it was to raise food, to hunt or to fish without reference to the needs of others.[16]

Karl Marx maintained that the source of drudgery in work is the alienation of humans from their own productivity. No explanation of the situation of the human person as "worker" is more definitive than Marx's and no theme is more central to his work; indeed, Peter Berger notes that "Marxian anthropology is . . . grounded in its concept of work . . . [and] man is defined and has historically defined himself by work."[17] Marx's analysis of human beings mired in alienated work, or drudgery, is captured well by Berger:

> Man is essentially the being that *produces*. He not only produces a world of his own, but, as he does this, he produces himself. Physical and mental work are inextricably connected in the process of human production. The tragedy of history, however, is that man has become alienated from his work, that is, the world that he has produced has become an autonomous and even hostile reality that confronts him as an alien thing. Alienation separates man from the products of his work, from his fellow men, and finally from himself. Under the conditions of alienated work, man works, not in order to fulfill himself (the anthropologically "correct" mode of working), but by necessity and in order to survive.[18]

David Riesman identifies alienated workers as the "other directed person(s)" and associates their alienation with the "break in consciousness" during the industrial revolution that effectively severed the relationship, both structurally and psychologically, between work and play or leisure:

> [The] "break in consciousness" between work and socialized play begins during the industrial revolution [and] has been completed. . . . work is irksome and if it cannot be evaded it can be reduced. In the old days the shadings between work and leisure were hard to distinguish. In modern life the idea is to minimize the unpleasant aspects of work as much as possible by pleasant distractions (wall colors, music, rest periods), and to hasten away as quickly as possible, uncontaminated by work and unimpaired by its arduousness.[19]

The perceptions of work as drudgery and of work and leisure as opposites replaced a classical perspective and an earlier psychological framework that gloried in leisure (though neither technological nor social patterns provided leisure opportunity for any but the few). Sloth, in this tradition, was not associated with being at rest, or working with such grace (or "technique" as Ryan says) that work seemed to lose its "laboriousness" and appeared to watching co-workers as laziness. In medieval tradition sloth is associated with the state of being incapable of leisure. Building on Aristotle's assertion in the *Metaphysics* that "not everything that is more difficult is necessarily more meritorious," Aquinas wrote, "The essence of virtue consists in the good rather than the difficult." In his modern classic, *Leisure, the Basis of Culture*, Joseph Pieper summarizes the tradition:

> At the zenith of the Middle Ages . . . it was held that sloth and restlessness, "leisurelessness," the incapacity to enjoy leisure, were all closely connected; sloth was held to be the source of restlessness and the ultimate cause of "work for work's sake."[20]

The basis of this wonderful and urgent insight rests on the proper understanding of sloth. Unlike the modern association of sloth with laziness, and the concomitant tendency to associate laziness with those who are not "laboring" endlessly, "the medieval view [of *acedia*, or sloth] means a man renounces the claim implicit in his human dignity . . . despair from weakness . . . not giv[ing] the consent of his will to his own being." According to Pieper, in this understanding "the contrary of *acedia* is not the spirit of work in the sense of the work of everyday, of earning one's living; it is man's happy and cheerful affirmation of his own being, his acquiescence in the world and in God—which is to say love."[21]

Theologian Dorothee Sölle evokes much the same, sad image of alienated, leisureless workers in her discussion of work as "treadmill" in her book, *To Work and To Love*.[22] Using the metaphor of work as treadmill, Sölle perceives that much of the work in which humans engage is alienating because it severs the worker from the overall plan, from novelty, from time, and from others: "The worker does not envision the work, does not plan the product he or she creates. . . . The daily cycle never changes [and there is] no control over time . . . an important part of a person's experience of freedom." Sölle applauds Pope John Paul II's encyclical letter on the priority of persons in all work, but concludes that under the conditions in which many humans work there is an alienation from one another based on the priority of production over persons, of what is made over who makes it. There are, in effect, no "fellow workers." Thus, much labor at the treadmill "destroys any sense of good work, in terms of self expression, relatedness to neighbor and reconciliation with nature." This alienation from the pleasure of work and "good work" is further aggravated by "wage slavery," which prompts us "to evaluate work according to salary. Good work pays more, inferior work pays less. No matter that the job is meaningless, injurious to others, inimical to oneself."

Sölle's analysis echoes that of the classical sociologist, Emil Durkheim. In *On the Division of Labor in Society*, Durkheim speaks of the "anomic work" that accompanies high specialization in the division of labor in modern industrial societies. Commenting on Durkheim's use of the term "anomia," Peter Berger defines it as "a state in which individuals have lost their social rootage and feel abandoned in an alien world."[23]

Eric Fromm, writing of the fundamental difference between traditional and modern work, points to much the same anomic circumstance or potential:

> Whether a carpenter makes a table or a goldsmith a piece of jewelry, whether the peasant grows his corn, or the painter paints a picture, in all types of creative work, the worker and his object become one, man unites himself with the world in the process of creation. This, however,

holds true only for produce work. In the modern work process of a clerk, the worker on the endless belt, little is left of this uniting quality of work. The worker becomes an appendix to the machine or to the bureaucratic organization. He has ceased to be he—hence no union takes place beyond that of conformity.[24]

There is a hint of the more sinister dimensions of the modern problem of alienated work in Fromm's reference to the workers' loss of being—"he has ceased to be he"—when subsumed in the "bureaucratic organization." This deeply rooted and pervasive social antagonism operates imperceptibly in the way modern work is organized. What Berger has called Thorstein Veblen's "peculiarly American modification of Marx's conception" helps explain this element of the problem. Writing at the turn of this century, Veblen said the alienation of modern work arises from antagonism between "confidence men" and "marks": those who "live by their mouths" and those who "live by their hands." The problem is the "one-upsmanship," as Berger characterizes it, of "ownership and salesmanship" over "workmanship."[25]

More recently, Robert Howard has performed an extraordinary service in calling attention to the way in which work within large corporate structures expands in influence to dominate every feature of the corporate worker's life, and does so in an apparently benevolent fashion that masks the elements of control and uniformity. Howard begins his book, *Brave New Workplace*, by describing the mood and ambience of a large corporate headquarters in the Silicon Valley: ". . . silence broken only by the gentle gurgling of fountains . . . muted music . . . lavish indoor tropical garden [with the] employee cafeteria right off [it with] . . . green marble floors and tables [and] chairs of powder blue crushed velvet and bronze. . . . health and fitness center . . . with saunas, whirlpool . . . racquetball courts, a running track . . . [and] exercise room. . . ." And one of the "nine full-time members of the Health and Fitness Center Staff" assures Howard: "We want to make people feel that this is their thing. That produces a good feeling about [name of the company]—that [name of the corporation] cares."[26]

Howard cites Robert Reich speaking of the dream of cooperative, healthy, corporate workers centering their lives on activities associated with the largess of their benevolent managers: "As geographic communities cease to have real social significance for many citizens, work places are becoming the center of social relationships . . . [and] . . . business enterprises are rapidly becoming the central mediating structures in American society."[27] Howard also offers his own assessment of the increasingly pervasive influence of corporate structures:

> The brave new work place is certainly a response to past criticisms and present uncertainties. But far from resolving the problems of work, it tends to disguise them, suppress them, and in the process create new problems (as yet unrecognized, let alone understood) even more difficult to address. For this corporate utopia for work denies the essential fact that work in America is a relationship of unequal power, that conflicts of interest are endemic to working life and that this new model of the corporation, much like the old, is founded on the systematic denial of influence and control to the large majority of working Americans.[28]

It is hard to read Howard's book without thinking of Herbert Marcuse's specter of the "one dimensional man" who lives in a "society without opposition," characterized by

> growing productivity and growing destruction; the brinkmanship of annihilation; the surrender of thought, hope and fear to the decisions of the powers that be; the preservation of misery in the face of unprecedented wealth. . . . [In such a society] the productive apparatus tends to become totalitarian to the extent to which it determines not only the socially needed occupations, skills and attitudes but also individual needs and aspirations . . . obliterat[ing] the distinction between private and public existence, between individual and social needs.[29]

The criticism that we are reviewing does not, however, rest solely on neo-Marxist indictments of modern industrial and corporate societies. The ultimate expression of alienation, which Marcuse speaks of as "happy consciousness," is dramatically, if sometimes whimsically, replicated in Rabbi Heschel's social critique.

Speaking about youth and education, themes of great concern to him, Heschel makes a distinction that is quite relevant to Howard's criticism of omnivorous corporate control and Marcuse's indictment of conformist society. It is the distinction and contrast between a "sense of belonging" and "a sense of significant being":

> The problem will not be solved by implanting in youth a sense of belonging. Belonging to a society that fails in offering opportunities to satisfy authentic human needs will not soothe the sense of frustration and rebellion. What youth needs is a sense of significant being."[30]

Heschel says that a sense of significant being is indivisible from a realization of suffering and an experience of challenge, experiences which the anesthetizing tendencies of modern corporate life seek to excise:

> We have denied our young people the knowledge of the dark side of life. They see a picture of ease, play and fun. That life includes hardship, illness, grief, even agony; that many hearts are sick with bitterness, resentfulness, envy—are facts of which many young people have hardly any awareness. They do not feel morally challenged, they do not feel called upon.[31]

In an utterly serious yet droll assessment of the relationship between facing problems and being a human being, Heschel shows in a most dramatic way the conflict between work which tempts the worker with comfortable conformity and the challenges of heroic being:

> . . . the greatness of man is that he faces problems. I would judge a person by how many deep problems he's concerned with. . . . A man with no problems . . . [is] an

idiot. A man has problems, and the more complicated, the richer he is the deeper his problems. This is our distinction, to have problems, to face problems. Life is a challenge not just a satisfaction. And the calamity of our times is to reduce life to pleasure only. . . . The greatness of life is experienced in facing problems rather than just having satisfaction. I would be frightened if I were to be ruled by a person who is satisfied, who has the answers to everything. In a very deep sense religion does two things. First of all, it's an answer to the ultimate problem of human existence . . . [and] it is a challenge to all answers. . . . If I look at the Bible, God is full of problems. . . . Look at the Bible: God is always wrestling with the problem of man; even God has problems. This is a deep ingredient of existence: problems! And the tragedy of our education today is we are giving such easy solutions: "be complacent, have peace of mind, everything is fine." No! Facing the challenge is the issue.[32]

In his encyclical letter *On Human Work*, John Paul II says that much work robs the worker of "all personal satisfaction and . . . incentive to creativity and responsibility, . . . reduc-[ing] man to the status of a slave."[33] Clearly, this slavery has many faces; it is present when work is overt drudgery on the treadmill, brutalizing and perceived as such. This slavery also operates, in perhaps its most efficient form, in the psychological manipulation of workers by corporate America's invitation to center their lives in the corporation. Whatever form alienating work takes, the experience cries out for the resistance. The energy and power to resist come from irony and contemplation.

WORK AND IRONY

Conrad Hyers' writings on the relationship between Christian faith and humor, including comedy, are an especially rich source of insight about our topic. In *The Comic Vision and the Christian Faith*, Hyers quotes the character Randall Patrick McMurphy, the truly sane man committed to a brutal mental institution in *One Flew Over the Cuckoo's Nest*. The character's commentary on the environment of the mental institution to which he is committed might well capture the situation and the effect of many work situations: "That's the first thing that got me about the place, there wasn't anybody laughing. I haven't heard a real laugh since I came through the door. . . . Man, when you lose your laugh, you lose your footing."[34]

Although Hyers does not dwell specifically on the role humor plays in mitigating the elements of drudgery and treadmill encountered in work life, in his wise examination of the relationship of humor and faithfulness we see how humor and faith fortify one another, enabling the humorous and faithful person to resist the terrible temptation of work-related seriousness and functionality, conflict and conformity. Hyers speaks of levels of humor, the first being a playful, childlike innocence, a "refusal to make sense, or make progress or make money all the time." Then there is humor "in the midst of conflict and anxiety, success and failure, faith and doubt. . . . humor com[ing] to terms . . . with the ambiguities and ambivalence of human existence . . . with absurdity, evil, suffering and death."[35] Hyers notes that "the very difficulties and disturbances that in real life [read: work-a-day life] may weary us, make us sick, throw us into an outrage, or have us shouting or crying or depressed are transformed by comic ritual into occasions for enjoyment if not hysterical laughter."[36]

That this humor is intimately related to contemplation, that it has the power to sanctify every moment of everyday, every frustration of work life and misunderstanding and conflict of family life, cannot be doubted. Of this "miracle of comedy" as he calls it, Hyers says:

> It is as though in some sacred sense this world for all its inequalities and this body for all its frailties and this time for all its inconsequentia is where one ought to be. It is as though life were intrinsically holy and that to fail to savor it, rejoice in it and be humored by it would be a great sacrilege.[37]

Gabriel Moran also examines the relationship between irony and work, though in a more explicit way. According to Moran, irony arises to cope with the reality of mortality: "Irony is a form of humor which merely recognizes our actual situation. . . . Humans have unlimited desires and elaborate plans but they have an extremely limited life span." In this function, irony is akin to mourning, for "the need to mourn [too] is a natural consequence of the sense of mortality. . . . Mourning is a non-verbal complement to ironic forms of speech."[38] Thus both irony and mourning are human responses to limitation; they are attitudes, skills, and gifts which enable us to cope with limitation—indeed, the ultimate expression of limitation—by embracing paradox, or as Zen thinkers would say, overcoming opposites. "Irony is the holding together of two attitudes: that human beings are the greatest things in the universe and that human beings are ridiculously small and vulnerable."[39]

In his theory of religious educational development, Moran identifies irony as one of the two personality strengths and educational qualities for which the maturing adult is striving. Prior to irony, the young adult is in thrall to "philosophy": continuing ideological striving, of a more or less rational character, to construct and construe a world. But if adults are able to move beyond this point to the educational stage that Moran designates as "journeying/inquiry," they will have laid aside rationalistic inquiry, accepted the paradoxical character of so many experiences in their journey, and seek to mature in a different sense, not as "controversialists but inquirers."[40] Moran concludes, "At this stage people . . . realize that their job may be important but that a job will not transform the universe. By staying at our life's work even as we become aware of its limitations, we make our job an education in irony."[41]

WORK AND CONTEMPLATION

If irony enables us to strive despite the finiteness of what can be achieved, contemplation enables us to see our work as transforming the universe. Together, irony and contemplation help workers achieve something like the mystical perspective on human work expressed by Teilhard de Chardin, for whom all our work is "eternalized" and each work "cherish[ed] . . . like children."[42] The contemplative traditions teach us that our work matters, matters immeasurably. Teilhard speaks to God of this work:

> No one lifts his little finger to do the smallest task unless moved, however obscurely, by the conviction that he contributing infinitesimally (at least indirectly) to the building of something definite—that is to say, to your work, my God. This may well sound strange or exaggerated to those who act without thoroughly scrutinizing themselves. And yet it is a fundamental law of their action. It requires no less than the pull of what men call the Absolute, no less than you yourself, to set in motion the frail liberty which you have given us.[43]

Similar insights are expressed through another tradition in Philip Kapleau's statement that "all work . . . is ennobling because it is seen as the expression of the immaculate Buddha—nature,"[44] or in Rabbi Heschel's conviction that "Labor is not only the destiny of man; it is endowed with divine dignity."[45] It is to the sublime importance of good work, of honoring our work and thereby honoring ourselves and honoring God, that Chuang Tsu points in his saying about "The Useless":

> Hui Tsu said to Chuang Tsu:
> "All your teaching is centered on what has no use."
>
> Chuang Tsu replied:
> "If you have no appreciation for what has no use
> You cannot begin to talk about what can be used.
> The earth, for example, is broad and vast
> But of all this expanse a man uses only a few inches
> Upon which he happens to be standing.
> Now suppose you suddenly take away
> All that he is not actually using
> So that, all around his feet a gulf

Yawns, and he stands in the Void,
With nowhere solid except right under each foot:
How long will he be able to use what he is using?"

Hui Tsu said:
"It would cease to serve any purpose."

Chuang Tsu concluded:
"This shows the absolute necessity
Of what has "no use.""[46]

Contemplative traditions not only affirm that our work, however modest, is quite simply of immeasurable value; they also assert that the performance of our work is the occasion of our sanctification, of becoming holy, of being at peace." In working in a peaceful way and working with a consciousness of the greatness of our "useless" work, we are agents of the "reconciliation with nature," in Dorothee Sölle's words. Sunyana Graef says of Buddhism, nature, and work:

The goal of Buddhist ecology . . . is a life of simplicity, conservation and self-restraint . . . actualized and expressed through the deeds of one's daily life. Such mundane chores as taking out the garbage, cooking a meal, cleaning the toilet and working in the garden are all occasions for the cultivation of spiritual awareness.[47]

In the same vein, the ancient Zen poet Hokoji suggests that there can be no peace at work nor love of the world unless we can sing: "How wonderfully supernatural, and how miraculous this! I draw water, and I carry fuel."[48] But this attitude toward work is not possible in the absence of the contemplative virtue of simplicity. This is the message at the heart of Shunryu Suzuki's classic, *Zen Mind Beginner's Mind*: to remain in spirit a beginner, simple and reverential toward the work, capable of being surprised by it. "In the beginner's mind there are many possibilities but in the expert's mind there are few. The goal of practice is always to keep our beginner's mind."[49]

To infuse our work with these contemplative qualities requires stubborn resolve, expressed gently and with grace. Many workers labor in contexts in which they and their work are merely instrumental to some other purposes, merely useful to ends of which the workers have little knowledge or loyalty, over which they have little power. They are paid simply "to remain silent and to conform to the rules of the game."[50] Yet any effort to define ourselves and our work as merely instrumental, as merely useful, must be resisted. For, as Teilhard says, "everything which diminishes my explicit faith in the heavenly value of the results of my endeavor, diminishes irredeemably my power to act."[51]

Contemplation is a form of resistance at a level of human life and response that is so elemental that the unreflective will not notice. Consider the revolutionary implications of these simple words of Shunryu Suzuki:

> Doing something is expressing our own nature. We do not exist for the sake of something else. . . . To cook, or to fix some food, is not preparation . . . it is practice. To cook is not just to prepare food for someone or for yourself; it is to express your sincerity.[52]

Or, in more straightforward prose, consider Thomas Merton's thoughts on usefulness and resistance. In the wonderful essay, "Rain and the Rhinoceros," Merton quotes Eugene Ionesco: "In all the cities of the world it is the same. The universal modern man is the man in a rush (i.e., the Rhinoceros), a man who has no time, who is a prisoner of necessity, who cannot understand that a thing might perhaps be without usefulness." Then, with characteristic directness, Merton adds: "We suffer all the needs that society demands we suffer because if we do not we lose our 'usefulness' in society—the usefulness of suckers."[53]

Now and only now is it admissible to speak of contemplation's gift of an increasing power to concentrate, to be competent at one's work. Before this point, mention of this quality might too easily be understood instrumentally, as

nothing more than a technique for improving "time man-
agement" in order to be more "useful." Now we can see
that the power of contemplation to promote concentration
effects a revolutionary self-possession of the time in which
we exist, the time which is constitutive of our selves, the
time that is robbed in brutal or at least boring work environments in which workers are treated merely as instruments.
As Solle says: "Our existence as beings in time requires that
we form and shape our time. It is like breathing in and
breathing out. Yet we are deprived of this very natural
aspect of our lives by most work."[54] Only now can Thich
Nhat Hanh's wonderful passage, "Washing the Dishes to
Wash the Dishes," be appreciated as a call for material and
spiritual liberation, an appreciation which is enhanced if one
is familiar with the Zen monk's remarkable heroism and
prophetic political commitments:

> While washing the dishes one should only be washing the
> dishes, which means that while washing the dishes one
> should be completely aware of the fact that one is wash-
> ing the dishes. At first glance, that might seem a little
> silly: why put so much stress on a simple thing? But that's
> precisely the point. The fact that I am standing there and
> washing these bowls is a wondrous reality. I'm being
> completely myself, following my breath, conscious of my
> presence, and conscious of my thoughts and actions.
> There's no way I can be tossed around mindlessly like a
> bottle slapped here and there on the waves. . . . If while
> washing dishes, we think only of the cup of tea that
> awaits us, thus hurrying to get the dishes out of the way
> as if they were a nuisance, then we are not "washing the
> dishes to wash the dishes." What's more, we are not alive
> during the time we are washing the dishes. In fact, we are
> completely incapable of realizing the miracle of life while
> standing at the sink. If we can't wash the dishes the
> chances are we won't be able to drink our tea either.
> While drinking the cup of tea, we will only be thinking of
> other things, barely aware of the cup in our hands. Thus
> we are *sucked away into the future—and we are incapable of*
> *actually living one moment of our lives.*[55]

The contemplative way of being and mode of consciousness enables the worker to reclaim pleasure in work, to breathe value into the simplest tasks, to savor the very simplicity of work and to approach the complexity of work with calm. But this contemplative attitude at work is not "opium," inducing sullen workers to put up with and thus cooperate in their own brutalization or boredom. The contemplative attitude arises from one of the healthier theologies of work that have held sway at one or another time in the history of Christianity. Unlike the "dual-eschatologist" view of work as "virtue-test on earth for world to come," or the "traditional ascetical [view of work] . . . as punishment for sin," the "Creationist" theology of work views the worker as "cooperating with God."[56]

Dorothee Sölle says that "the theology of the bourgeoisie deals with work under the themes of curse and hardship . . . [and] religion has served to accommodate people to meaningless work."[57] The roots of this theology lie in both Calvinism and Jansenism. Speaking of the influence of the former, Stanley Parker writes:

> The main legacy of Calvinism arises from its paradoxical command to deny the world but live in the world, to work hard to accumulate wealth but not to spend it on oneself. This is the foundation of the nineteenth century cult of work and the abhorrence of idleness and pleasure.[58]

And lest Protestantism take all the blame (or credit) for this earnest but dour assessment of work and fidelity, consider Francis Schüssler Fiorenza's analysis of how Jansenistic Catholicism promotes much the same values:

> The divine favor is seen [by the Jansenists] not so much in the rich and powerful as in the middle class and especially in their fidelity to obligations, their dedication to hard work and their earnest and self-sufficient attitude toward life. . . . The Jansenist attitude praise[s] work precisely because it is difficult, weary, monotonous, necessary and strenuous. Work unmasks the vanity of the world. It undercuts the human desire for pleasure. . .[it is] penance for sin.[59]

But truly contemplative workers know their work is not a curse, nor will they acquiesce in what Joe Holland calls the "instrumentalization of [their work] by viewing it mainly as a means to consumption."[60] Contemplative workers know that their time is precious, "eternalized" as Teilhard says, and that the work which they perform in time is part of God's timeless work. There is not only peace but also resistance and liberation in the heart of a worker in whose time God dwells. Rabbi Heschel describes this aspect of contemplative work and time beautifully:

> . . . there are hours which perish and hours which join the everlasting. . . . Humans hand over our time to God in the secrecy of single words. When anointed by prayer, a person's thoughts and deeds do not sink into nothingness, but merge into endless knowledge of an all-embracing God. We yield our thoughts [and works] to God who endowed us with a chain of days for the duration of our lives.[61]

WORK AND CONTEMPLATIVE FORMATION

The work of contemplative formation is a work of education. But while the educational efforts of the church entail some formation in prayer, these efforts almost never extend in a thoughtful and sustained way to work life or to the relationship between prayer and work. And the idea that pastoral educational services of a local religious community should be used to help clarify the paradoxical character of much adult experience and thus promote an ironic attitude would most probably be dismissed as an obscure, over-sophisticated notion.

If the organized efforts of local religious communities to promote a contemplative perspective on work are to have any real effect, they must begin with the acknowledgment that the work in which the adult[62] members of the religious community are engaged is very important to their lives. Certainly a compassionate and caring religious community is one which sustains members in sorrows associated with work and the loss of work and perhaps but to a lesser extent, helps members celebrate achievement at work. But in most religious communities the attention paid to people's work lives, both within and outside the home, is *ad hoc* and incidental. Sustained and broadscale efforts in preaching and education in a theology of work need to be made to help people through the joys and sorrows of their work lives. Pastoral educational leaders of local religious communities need to solicit expressions of feeling about work and its effects from the members of the community, and to allow for real and concrete theological reflection on the meaning of the limitations of our work and the relationship between work and prayer.

Moran's writings in religious educational theory are among the few which propose explicit connections between education, prayer, (especially in its contemplative expressions) and work. Moran considers work central to education: "Work is what life is concerned with, and in the richest sense of the word, work is the aim of all education."[63] He proposes an explicit task for the community's religious educational efforts:

> Religious education. . . . is the revitalization of one's job or ordinary task toward one's work or vocation. . . . Religious education from the standpoint of work is whatever affirms our job while reminding us that there is something greater to be accomplished in our lives.[64]

This definition contains a real and comprehensive agenda, and not simply *ad hoc* educational ministry as specific events in a person's work life call for support and consolation. Under its influence, religious educational leadership invites conversation about work, highlighting the difference between the jobs at which we labor and the nobility of the work of creation to which we are called. When members of the local religious community know that work is perceived as a crucial element in their efforts to be faithful, and when difficulties at work are regularly spoken of, then isolated housewives will be joined together in mutual support and frightened middle-aged men "mustering all their strength to get themselves through another ten to fifteen years on the job"[65] will know that there is a company of people to whom they may go to voice their anger and frustration.

Moran's notion, examined earlier, about the time of journeying/inquiry in which work is prominent and irony crucial can be more fully appreciated when seen in conjunction with what he believes is the next and final stage of religious educational development of the maturing adult, a stage characterized by the task of "centering" or being contemplative, "an attitude of peace, wholeness and centeredness."[66] The characteristic personality strength which Moran believes the person strives for at this time is leisure, "the stage at which we situate a fully developed self in a calmly accepted cosmos."[67] Here Moran brings his proposal for relating work and contemplation full circle. For while he believes that the final attainment of contemplative leisure is most often possible in the lives of older adults, he is nevertheless convinced that "the leisure attitude is possible on the job and off the job."[68]

Quite simply, the religious community has an essential role to play in connecting the ability to contemplate to the work lives of members. To be free of work as drudgery, treadmill, and alienation, to survive brutal work or work in the "grey region," to respond wisely in the face of work-related failure, the members of religious communities must encounter in these communities an explicit invitation to heal the pain of work and firm support to resist staying at meaningless work.

Freedom from meaningless work requires insight into a distinction that Parker Palmer has recently made between our acquired skills and our native gifts. Faced with the malaise of work life for many of its members, the religious community, he believes, should invite us to consider the distinction and to take joy in native gifts:

> The skills we are most aware of possessing are often those we have acquired only through long hours of study and practice, at considerable financial and personal cost. Precisely because these skills once cost us effort to acquire, and still cost us effort to employ, we are acutely aware of owning them. Ironically, these self-conscious skills are often not our leading strengths; if they were they would not be so effortful. But they are the strengths upon which we sometimes build our identities and our careers—though we build on an anxious, uncertain foundation. Meanwhile, our native, instinctive gifts either languish unused and unappreciated or get used unconsciously without being named or claimed.[69]

The religious community invites its members to escape meaningless work by training them in contemplative prayer. Only the religious community can provide an option to the vacuous choice (which some workers consider the only choice) between job and free time. Moran says: "What the twentieth century seems to demand is that the first half of life [or the first five days of the week] be disciplined, rational and productive, while the other half [or Saturday and Sunday] be undisciplined, irrational and consumerist."[70] Moran's criticism is similar to that of Jacques Ellul, who says in *The Technological Society* that leisure time has become "a mechanized time and is exploited by techniques which although different from those of man's ordinary work are as invasive, exacting and leave man no more free than labor itself."[71] Moran concludes his observation about job and free time by saying, "People are not free merely by being off the job but by the gradual integration of active and receptive modes of living" This integrated mode of living is contemplative; for this task, "The Churches have an historic mission today to be zones of quiet."[72]

POSTSCRIPT: WORK AND HEROISM

In *The Myth of the Birth of the Hero*, Otto Rank says that in our very first work, being born, we are heroic; such work is difficult and requires spirit and courage.[73] The notion of heroism keeps coming to mind while reflecting on irony, work, and contemplation. So much work diminishes the person's sense of dignity and nobility, the sense, as Meister Eckhart sang out, that each of us is an aristocrat! Without a contemplative attitude promoting a sense of our worth, our life experience can level us and makes us think we are average, able to fulfill the human need for heroic action only in pitifully superficial ways. Ernest Becker evokes this situation when he says, "The debt to life has to be paid somehow; one has to be a hero in the best way he can—even if only for his skill at the pinball machine."[74]

But we are not average; as Rabbi Heschel says: "In the eyes of the world, I am an average man. But to my heart I am not average. To my heart I am of great moment. The challenge I face is how to actualize the quiet eminence of my own being."[75] "Comic heroism," as Hyers calls it, will save us from the sadness of being made to feel average and from being made average. Hyers prefers this kind of heroism to the tragic variety:

> Tragic heroism has a Promethean/Oedipal air of Adolescence about it. Comic heroism with its flexibility and inclination to compromise, its playfulness and delight in ambiguity, its knowing wink and lighter countenance is the more mature form.[76]

Contemplation will save us from passivity and resignation in our work, as well as from distraction, for it will instruct us in the nobility of our work and in resistance to bad work by convincing us that our work is part of God's play in God's garden. As Merton says: "The Lord plays and diverts Himself in the garden of His creation and if we could let go of our own obsession with what we think is the meaning of it all, we might be able to hear His call and follow Him in His mysterious, cosmic dance."[77]

Such a co-worker or playmate or dance partner of God's is surely a hero. The awareness of our true selves which comes from contemplation, an awareness which is like "digging deep into the soil until we reach a hidden source of fresh water . . . our true mind, the source of understanding and compassion,"[78] is the means to this heroic perspective on our lives and our works, and is liberation from frustration, irritation, anger, and alienation at work.

Chapter Five

"Sacred Dwellings":
Growing Up and Being Peace
in Contemplative Homes

The family, like the meditative and contemplative traditions, promises freedom. The ideal of the modern family is that of a place for the growth of personal freedom joined to a sense of responsibility. Sadly, few in number are those who experience the liberation of contemplative being, with its promise of both freedom and responsibility, in the context of family life. In *Sacred Dwellings*, her remarkable book on the possibilities of creating a truly contemplative family life, Wendy Wright says that families are "seen as either a potential hindrance to individual development. . .or. . .as entities to which all individuals must be submerged."[1]

Psychological and psychiatric assessment of borderline dysfunctional families supports concern for individual development in families. In their study of psychological health and dysfunction of families and family members, Beavers and Hampson state that borderline families "are characterized by chaotic and overt power struggles, with persistent (though ineffective) efforts to build and maintain stable patterns of dominance and submission."[2] Samuel Butler's appraisal of oppressive and forced solidarity rooted in sentimentality about the family is as instructive today as it was when he wrote it in the seventeenth century: "I believe that more unhappiness comes from this source than from any other—I mean from the attempt to prolong family connection unduly and to make people hang together artificially who would never naturally do so."[3]

The family is the first, indispensable environment for the cultivation of contemplative being. It is the human and physical environment in which either such being is nurtured or a trajectory of scattered and wounded being is established. An essential feature of contemplative being discussed in chapter 3 is being delivered to ourselves as subjects. Maria Harris connects family life with this elemental condition for growth in contemplative being when she writes that "the family, because it is a primary place of suffering and undergoing as well as a place of joy and celebration, is in the unique position to give human beings one of the first experiences of *receptivity to themselves*."[4] Such receptivity to self is linked to contemplation by Augustine who writes: "Descend into thyself; go into the secret chamber of thy mind. If thou be far from thyself, how cans't thou be near to God."[5] Consider these observations alongside those of Beavers and Hampson, as they conclude their description of borderline dysfunctional families: "Individual family members have little ability to attend to and accept emotional needs in themselves and others."[6]

To speak of the family as the environment for cultivating contemplative being is to speak of establishing a ground for nonviolence. Yet we all know that families are beset by conflict. As Dick Westley writes: "At the heart of every human family is the basic clash of wills, the conflict of differing value systems, the struggle between dependence and autonomy, and, most significantly, the challenge of relating sexually."[7]

To speak of the family as the environment for cultivating contemplative being is also to speak of establishing a ground for growth in self-worth: the sense, as D. T. Suzuki says, that one's life is an inimitable masterpiece. Yet the literature of psychology, especially family theory, is replete with clinical descriptions of frustration of self-worth linked to family patterns of domination and subordination, anger and frustration born of role expectations that undermine self- affirmation. Ernest Boyer writes, "The demons of the spirituality of the family, and in fact of community in general, are the frustrations, anger and despair that again and again appear in a life lived for others."[8] And in her wise commentary on what she calls *Christian Uncertainties*, Monica Furlong says:

> The closest and often the most fraught of family relationships is that between parents and children. All loving relationships have one crucial problem to face—that of the freedom of those related; and it is particularly difficult in the case of parents and children just because children have been helpless and dependent for so long that parents get into the habit of being in a position of strength and authority.[9]

Again, to speak of the family as the environment for cultivating contemplative being is to speak of establishing a ground for compassion which extends beyond circles of intimacy to embrace other neighbors. But the family can block the expansion of compassion, either because no such compassionate pattern is established or because a pseudo-compassion is reserved for family members only. Warnings about the dangers of blocking compassion were part of the message of Jesus; they are echoed in Stanley Hauerwas' cogent criticism of family hubris.[10] Freud, too, noted that "the more closely members of a family are attached to one another, the more often do they tend to cut themselves off from others and the more difficult it is for them to enter the wider circle of life."[11]

Finally, to speak of the family as the environment for cultivating contemplative being is to speak of establishing a ground for liberation from suffering. Such liberation is the end or purpose of contemplation, religion, and all forms of communal existence. Yet, as Wendy Wright addresses her readers at the beginning of *Sacred Dwellings*, "Most of your families are scarred to one degree or another by death, dis-ease, alcoholism, drug addiction, violence, spouse-battering, child abuse, lack of communication, quarrelling between generations." While contemplative being has to do with being "collected" and "present," family life is dominated by the "pressure of succeeding, . . . overwhelmed with financial worries, seduced by consumerist views[s] of ultimate happiness . . . [and its members] absent from one another's lives because of the sheer number of commitments."[12] Mary Perkins Ryan painted an equally powerful portrait of the scattered and absent family in the mid-fifties when she wrote of the "family week" with its "strain of the five working days, the weekend filled with odd jobs, violent amusement and the *relaxation of exhaustion.*"[13]

For all the good will and intelligence that go into formal initiatives of the church to help nurture healthy and religiously formative families, it is hard to disagree with Wright's assessment that these programs do little to enhance the family as environment for contemplative being. Indeed,

> . . . the very emphasis of the Church's family programming, especially when it is geared for each age and interest group, becomes a force that fragments the family. . . . [and encourages family members] to import "churchy" rituals or prayers into their homes hoping this will impart religious meaning to their shared life.[14]

In our reflection on contemplative being and human development in families we need to ask, What might a healthy family life look like? Consider the clinical description of "optimal families" in Beavers and Hampson's *Successful Families.* Optimal families are those in which

> intimacy is sought and usually found, a high level of respect for individuality and the individual perspective is the norm, and capable negotiation and communicational clarity are the results. There is a strong sense of individuation with clear boundaries, hence conflict and ambivalence (at the individual level) are handled directly, overtly and (usually) negotiated efficiently. The hierarchical struc-

ture of the family is well defined and acknowledged by the members. Yet there is also flexibility—a high level of adaptation to individual development, stress and individuation which reflects morphogenetic forces balancing the system. In fact, in later years of the evolution of the family—a process acknowledged throughout the course—the family becomes a loosely connected, lovingly respectful group of equal adults with another generation emerging.[15]

Functional relations, intimacy, freedom, individuation or healthy individualism in the form of self-worth and attribution of worth by others, communicational competence, appropriate order, flexibility, and growth: we would say members of such families "have it all together." Members of such families are collected not dispersed, whole not fractured; thus it is not reaching very far to characterize the "optimal family" as a ground of formation in contemplative being. And if Beavers and Hampson's description seems to some to propose a norm that is excessively individualistic (after all, how about a little suffering, guilt, and dysfunction for the sake of family solidarity), consider their assumption that appropriate "individuation" is healthy alongside the ancient Buddhist story of the father and daughter, a tale recounted by Nhat Hanh:

> There is a story in the Pali canon about a father and a daughter who performed in the circus. The father would place a very long bamboo stick on his forehead, and his daughter would climb to the top of the stick. When they did this, people gave them some money to buy rice and curry to eat. One day the father told the daughter "My dear daughter, we have to take care of each other. You have to take care of your father, and I have to take care of you, so that we will be safe. Our performance is very dangerous." Because if she fell both would not be able to earn their living. If she fell, then broke her leg, they wouldn't have anything to eat. "My daughter, we have to take care of each other so we can continue to earn our living."

The daughter was wise. She said, "Father, you should say it this way: Each one of us has to take care of himself or herself, so that we can continue to earn our living. Because during the performance you take care of yourself, you take care of yourself only. You stay very stable, very alert. That will help me. And if when I climb I take care of myself, I climb very carefully, I do not let anything wrong happen to me. That is the way you should say it, Father. You take good care of yourself, and I take good care of myself. In that way we can continue to earn our living."

[Nhat Hanh concludes:] The Buddha agreed that the daughter was right.[16]

CONTEMPLATIVE BEING AND RESPECT FOR CHILDREN

Faced with a picture of conflictual, manipulative, violent, and scattered family life in which there is more absence from than presence to one another, what can be said about efforts to build families that are grounds of contemplative being? We can begin as "vagabonds of the obvious" by insisting that first adult members of families must seek to change themselves into contemplatives. Annette Hollander points to this when, speaking of a child's spiritual life, she says, "As parents we cannot 'transform' our children, but to the extent that we can *train our consciousness* we can support [the spiritual life] unfolding in our children."[17] Hollander's reference to training our consciousness parallels that of Monica Furlong when she speaks of inner growth: "As the children grow . . . so must the parents, just as miraculously and demandingly, except that theirs is an *inner growth*."[18] Pope John Paul II points to the same transformation of adult consciousness in family life when he speaks in *Familiaris Consorto* of the familial need for "a profoundly restored *covenant with divine wisdom*."[19]

For the adult members of the family, changing ourselves entails the serious (though never solemn or feverishly

dutiful) effort to live a "devout life." Francis de Sales' masterpiece, *Philothea, or An Introduction to the Devout Life*, deserves
to be noted at this point. It isn't difficult to relate de Sales'
notion of true devotion expressing itself in family life and the
idea of the family as a ground of contemplative being when—
but only when—adult members seek to change themselves
by living a devout life. We read that with true devotion
"domestic peace is assured, conjugal love strengthened, fidelity to our [God] more closely treasured, and all occupations
rendered more acceptable and agreeable."[20] De Sales insists
that the devout life is available to all, a revolutionary notion
which parallels the assumption expressed in this book that
contemplation is not solely a monastic phenomenon or meditation an obscure preoccupation of those attracted to esoteric
practices. Indeed, de Sales maintains that "it is not merely an
error but a heresy to suppose that a devout life is banished
from the soldier's camp, the merchant's shop, the prince's
court, or the domestic hearth."[21]

Respect for the child is the first functional expression of
"changed consciousness," an "inner life," a "covenant with
wisdom," and "true devotion" in the lives of adult members
of the family striving to make family life a ground of contemplative formation. Such respect is not found in allowing
children to become addicted to consumption of unnecessary
and often undesirable trinkets, or in parents abdicating the
exercise of authority that might bring order, the acceptable
hierarchy of persons and values to which Beavers and
Hampson refer. True respect of the child available to the
contemplative parent exists at two levels, one general, the
other more specific.

The general respect for the child is a function of that
larger "respect for persons" which R. S. Peters identifies as
one of the "rational passions" and which he links to Hume's
notion of the "sentiment of humanity." It is treating others
as ends not as means.[22] In contrast to this notion, we have
Max Horkheimer's chilling, Freudo-Marxist, sketch of the
child of the middle class family:

The child's self will is to be broken and the innate desire
for free development of his drives and potentialities
replaced by an internalized compulsion toward duty. Submission to the categorical imperative of duty has been
from the beginning a conscious goal of the bourgeois
family.[23]

Neo-Marxist or not, who can deny the accuracy of
Horkheimer's point about the torrent of aggression directed
against children in the name of duty? The barely disguised
criticism of Kant in this quote is worth considering, for it
was Kant who understood religion as the recognition of all
our duties as divine commands. The moralism and psychic
violence directed at children in "religious homes" (or super-
markets for that matter) under the influence of this anthem
cannot be exaggerated. Such a notion of religion is, not coin-
cidentally, antagonistic to the contemplative or mystical
dimension.

This general lack of respect for the child expresses itself
in a program which robs children of childhood. Murray, in
the film "A Thousand Clowns," rebels against such a program in the form of insistence that he "come back to reality," by saying that he will do so "only as a tourist."
Matthew Fox identifies the excessive call to duty and its
adverse effects on both children and older persons when he
accuses the leadership of the Holy Office and those responsible for (duty bound to) orthodoxy of "adultism." This is
also the robbery of childhood to which Wordsworth refers:

> Heaven lies about us in our infancy;
> Shades of the prison house begin to
> close upon the growing boy.
> At length the man perceives it die away
> and fade into the light of common day.[24]

Respect for the child in a family that is a ground for
contemplative being is likewise spoken of with eloquence
and feeling by Ralph Waldo Emerson. His perspective
makes it clear that it is only the parent who is growing as a

contemplative who can exercise such respect: "Respect your child; be not too much his parent. *Intrude not on his solitude.*"[25] Henry Nelson Wieman's analysis makes the link between contemplative being and respect for the child even clearer. Writing of differing modes of cognition and having assessed what he calls "practical" and "theoretical" cognition, Wieman writes:

> We may cognize a child in the practical attitude. We study how to deal with him so as to get him to do our will with the least sound and fury. Or being a student of genetic psychology, we consider him with a view to testing some theory. But if we love the child we may sometimes *contemplate him.* In so doing we may keep true to all that practice and theory has revealed about him. But our attitude toward him is very different and what we discern in him far exceeds what enters our minds as we theorize or practically deal with him. Far more of the concrete total individuality of the child comes to our knowledge when we contemplate him.[26]

The foundation of respect for the child lies in acknowledging that childhood, as Edward Robinson says, is "an element of the whole person,"[27] and not a manifestation of deficient adulthood. Those who contemplate the child, perceiving "far more of the total individuality" of that child, will not make the mistake that robs children of childhood. Here we come to the more specific level of respect for the child: acknowledging that children have rich spiritual and religious lives.

Failure to acknowledge the richness of the religious life of children is the basis of moralistic and unimaginative early childhood religious socialization, an experience which renders the possibility of contemplative being remote. Jerome Berryman addresses this problem, asking, "Why can't religious education teach children (and adults) how to pierce the conventions of language to experience the creator directly?"[28] Berryman's criticism is directly related to the possibilities of contemplative being: early religious education based on the assumption that children do not have a religious life until they can think about having a "religion" fails to notice, encourage, and cultivate the experiences of awe and thanksgiving that are the ground in which the possibility of such being rests. Moran notes, "'Having a religion' may indeed only be recognizable in the upper years of elementary school, but being religious is a condition known to every child."[29] It is to their radical capacity for awe and therefore—eventually—for contemplation that G. K. Chesterton referred when he said, "A child of seven is excited by being told that Tommy opened a door and saw a dragon. But a child of three is excited by being told that Tommy opened a door."[30]

Rabbi Heschel's description of awe leaves little doubt that where this spirit is extinguished in children, the capacity for contemplative being is destroyed:

> Awe is an intuition for the dignity of all things, a realization that things not only are what they are but also stand, however remotely, for something supreme. Awe is a sense for the transcendence, for the reference everywhere to mystery beyond all things. It enables us to perceive in the world intimations of the divine . . . to sense the ultimate in the common and simple; to feel in the rush of the passing the stillness of the eternal.[31]

> The ineffable inhabits the magnificent and the common, the grandiose and the tiny facts of reality alike. Some people sense this quality at distant intervals in extraordinary events; others sense it in ordinary events, in every fold, in every nook; day after day, hour after hour. To them things are bereft of triteness. Slight and simple as things may be—a piece of paper, a morsel of bread, a word, a sigh—they hide a never ending secret: a glimpse of God? Kinship with the spirit of being? An eternal flash of the will?[32]

The contemplative parent must acknowledge, revere, and cultivate the child's capacity for awe by providing, in Moran's words, "aesthetic form, stable environment, and personal warmth that protect the religiousness of the child's experience."[33]

The child is disrespected and the capacity for contemplative being is diminished by impatient adults who consider the religious imaginations of children as, in Robinson's words, "poetic fancy" to be easily dismissed. Keith Egan agrees that children experience the most profound human emotions: "What children know best when they come to school are love, hate, joy, fear, good, bad."[34] From his many years of working with sick and terminally ill children at the Texas University Medical Center, Berryman is able to correct the false assumption of many adults that children do not experience the existential questions of "death, aloneness, meaninglessness, and the threat of freedom." He speaks eloquently:

I was with children as they helped each other prepare for death when their parents and other significant adults were not able to help them. Some children even helped their parents cope with their death as they were dying.[35]

These authors are unanimous in ascribing the disrespect of the spiritual and religious lives of children to the rationalistic and moralistic focus in the work on cognition and moral judgment of Jean Piaget and of Ronald Goldman, a major interpreter of Piaget's thought in religious education. Robinson says, "The starting point of all Piaget's thought about childhood is the incapacity of children to see the world as adults see it," adding that much of the claim that children do not see the world "realistically actually rests on a fact that children do not see the world in wholly materialistic terms."[36] Commenting on the work of Ronald Goldman, especially Goldman's notorious assertion that "religious insight generally begins to appear between the ages of twelve or thirteen," Gabriel Moran says:

The severe limitations of a Piagetian approach to religious education were demonstrated by the work of Ronald Goldman in the 1960s. . . . The troublesome or even *shocking* thing was Goldman's use of the word *religious*. The child of five to seven was called pre-religious; seven to eleven was the sub-religious phase. Up until adolescence, religious education was still something that children were being prepared for.[Moran quotes Goldman:] "The change from concrete to abstract modes of thought appears to become possible in religious thinking about the age of thirteen years. The adolescent is now in what I call his religious stage of development, in which he is intellectually ready to apprehend what is the Christian faith." Evident in this statement is the conflating of *Christian* and *religious*. Related to that problem is the assumption that religious education means apprehending the "Christian faith" by abstract modes of thought.[37]

The thinking and practice which Moran criticizes delays or cancels the possibility in later life of openness to the contemplative dimension.

The disdain of childhood religiousness is paralleled by the general disdain of the mystical to which William James pointed: "The words 'mysticism' and 'mystical' are often used as terms of mere reproach, to throw at any opinion which we regard as vague and vast and sentimental, and without a base in either fact or logic."[38] Yet James' definition of the mystical, like Robinson's research, suggests that mystical experiences are available to the child, for they are "states of insight into depths of truth unplumbed by the discursive intellect. They are illuminations, revelations, full of significance and importance, all inarticulate though they remain; and as a rule carry with them a curious sense of authority for aftertime."[39]

Awe and subjectivity of a certain kind need to be fostered to grow. The disrespect of children, their premature and often excessive subordination to duty, the dismissal of their imaginations and of their feeling for life's most profound mysteries, leave little hope for the growth of contemplative adults. Along these lines, Gabriel Marcel said of himself:

I tend to become increasingly profane in relation to a certain mystery of my self to which access is more and more

strictly forbidden me. I should add that this unquestion-
ably comes about in so far as the child that I used to be,
and that I should have remained were I a poet, dies a little more each day.[40]

And Sean O'Faolain wrote, "If the boy within us ceases
to speak to the man who enfolds him, the shape of life is
broken."[41]

I have been suggesting that presence to and wonder for
mystery constitute contemplative being. If these qualities are
to take root and grow, children must be allowed and encouraged to preserve the child within them.

CONTEMPLATIVE BEING AND SUPPORT
FOR YOUTH AND YOUNG ADULTS

The American Psychiatric Society defines adolescence as

a chronological period beginning with the physical and
emotional processes leading to sexual and psychological
maturity and ending at an ill-defined time when the individual achieves independence and social productivity.
The period is associated with rapid physical, psychological and social changes.[42]

Not much help really, so consider this more evocative
sketch by Erik Erikson:

There is a "natural" period of uprootedness in human life:
adolescence. Like a trapeze artist, the young person in the
middle of vigorous motion must let go of his safe hold on
childhood and reach out for a firm grasp on adulthood,
depending for a breathless interval on a relatedness
between the past and the future and on the reliability of
those he must let go of and those who will receive him.[43]

For youth and young adults alike, the adult community
in a variety of familial forms must be contemplative precisely
in its capacity to exercise what Wendy Wright refers to as the
family "discipline of welcoming and letting go." The profound welcoming I have in mind here, and which I have

written about in an essay entitled "Hospitality as Paradigm for Youth Ministry,"[44] is only available to the centered and secure person. "Welcoming," Wright adds, employing a metaphor synonymous with contemplative being, "is to love with purity of heart." Letting go, as we have seen, is an equally adequate summary of the actual, functioning state of consciousness of one who is contemplative. The whole discipline of welcoming and letting go "is very much a part of spiritual maturity, to being reformed into a closer likeness to . . . God."[45]

The vulnerability of adolescence should evoke sympathy in the adult community. Erikson speaks of it as the time of the "ideological seeking after an inner coherence and a durable set of values"; the time of striving to develop fidelity, "the ability to sustain loyalties freely pledged in spite of the inevitable contradictions of value systems."[46] It is a time in which the young person needs confirming adults.

Gabriel Moran refers to this time as a time of "philosophical" striving, an idea similar to what Erikson has in mind in speaking of adolescent efforts to forge an "ideology." The proper response to such a time is calm, receptivity, and understanding. Young people are experiencing nothing less than death: "Youth is primarily an experience of death—the death of childhood."[47]

The contemplative adult community will embrace adolescents, providing them with the "moratorium" which they require: "Adolescence is . . . a psychological moratorium affording an individual some moments to mend the self-concept, a pause to practice roles and time to transform oneself into committed adults."[48] Such a community will provide what Maria Harris calls a certain "genuine solitude," "the opportunity for the young to be 'watchers' observing life without judging it, getting the feel of it and sensing it flows and rhythm."[49] Adults in a contemplative community "can provide a safety zone where ideas can be played with rather than overpowering the young with an alternative ideology."[50]

Where are the confirming adults? Where are the adults who can be relied upon to behave with calm and sympathetic understanding, continuing to welcome while exercising the discipline of letting go? Where are the adults who provide moratorium, genuine solitude, safety zones? Where are adults who practice purity of heart? Where are the holy adults? Perhaps they are scarce because as children they were not formed in families that provided a ground for contemplative being. Rabbi Heschel believes that reverence for parents is the only path in life to reverence itself:

> Reverence for parents is the fundamental form of reverence, for in the parent is incarnated the mystery of man's coming into being. Rejection of the parent is a repudiation of the mystery. Only a person who lives in a way which is compatible with the mystery of human existence is capable of evoking reverence in the child. The basic problem is the parent, not the child.[51]

And perhaps these adults are not here because they are not challenged and encouraged by the church to live a contemplative life. Is the church, in Moran's words, "a place of contemplative prayer, rhythmically related to intense social action"? Do we, as church, "provide content for the ready loyalty of youth"?[52] Are we worthy of the "affiliative" exercise of faith which Westerhoff sees youth desiring?[53]

Sharon Parks points to the essentially contemplative purpose of the religious community in discussing the "vocation of religion" and its attraction to young adults: "The purpose of religion is to reveal a consciousness of being created for and beckoned into faithful participation in the delight, demands and sacred mystery of the everyday."[54] It is questionable whether the church fulfills this vocation in great measure, or whether, on the contrary, it participates in what Rabbi Heschel considers the general lines along which culture and religion decline in nobility and in doing so alienate youth. It is clear from Heschel's commentary that the problem of culture and religion is very much related to the absence of contemplative values:

The problem of our youth is not youth. The problem is the spirit of our age: denial of transcendence, the vapidity of values, emptiness in the heart, the decreased sensitivity to the imponderable quality of the spirit, the collapse of communication between the realm of tradition and the inner world of the individual. The central problem is that we do not know how to think, how to pray, how to cry, how to resist the deceptions of too many persuaders.[55]

From a somewhat different point of departure, Johannes Metz challenges members of the church to stop substituting rigorism for radicalism:

My starting assumption is that the reason for the church's loss of appeal is not that it demands too much from people, but that it offers, in fact, too little challenge. . . . If the church were more "radical" in the gospel sense, it would probably not need to be so "rigorous" in the legal sense. Rigorism springs more from fear, radicalism from freedom, the freedom of Christ's call.[56]

Much but not all of what has been said of youth and their need for confirming contemplative persons and contemplative environments can be said of young adults, though one hesitates to leave the impression that young adulthood is being treated as an appendage to the study of adolescence. Studies such as Sharon Park's *The Critical Years* encourage us to look carefully at the unique dynamics of young adulthood, building on earlier insights such as Carl Jung's idea of young adulthood as the second stage of "life's morning" and Erik Erikson's studies of young adulthood and identity formation in *Young Man Luther*.

When defined as persisting through much of one's thirties, even a flexible notion of young adulthood—one which avoids the mechanism and smugness of some development thinking—evokes images of great activity, the most active years. This is the time for what Jung calls "psychic birth" and creative adjustment of identity in a complex world, "the establishment of the ego in the world."[57] Gabriel Moran says that "religious attitudes in young adulthood are embodied in the way people act as parents, workers, friends and citizens."[58] Neitzsche's wonderful allegory contained in the section on the "Three Metamorphoses" in *Thus Spoke Zarasthrustra* sheds light on this feature of young adulthood as well. No longer a camel accepting the burden of values into which they have been socialized, young adults are the lion in the desert:

> In the loneliest desert, however, the second metamorphosis occurs: here the spirit becomes a lion who would conquer his freedom and be master in his own desert. Here he seeks out his last master: he wants to fight him and his last god; for ultimate victory he wants to fight with the great dragon.
>
> Who is the great dragon whom the spirit will no longer call lord and god? "Thou shalt" is the name of the great dragon. But the spirit of the lion says, "I will."[59]

Young adults are not yet the child— Nietzsche's metaphor for the perfection of humanity, Erikson's for the fullness of personality development, and ours for the contemplative person—therefore, they have need of sponsorship in contemplation. It would be a great mistake to side-step the hunger of young adults for peace and calm amidst the tumult of "making their way" and to justify this by reference to the developmental priority of action in young adulthood. The "spiritualization of nature" in the middle years to which Jung refers is not automatic. The world is strewn with middle-aged persons who lost a sense of the inner life during the period of their lives in which nature and culture encouraged striving aggressively for "success."

Sharon Parks captures the need to sponsor young adults in the practice of meditative or contemplative being, noting that the emerging self of the young adult says, in effect, "I am aware that I am responsible for who I am becoming."[60] The capacity for reflectivity implied in this remark is a function of contemplative being.

Commenting on the shift in young adulthood from "Superego God" to a "Personal God," John Shea, O.S.A. says:

> Perhaps the most crucial element in the transition from the "Superego God" to the "Personal God" of young adulthood is the opportunity to give expression to one's unique, inner experience of God. Up to this point the emphasis has been on "Who God is," and now there is a shift to a concentration on "Who God is *for me*.[61]

Life cannot be lived in a manner which expresses "one's unique inner experience of God" apart from the practice of contemplative being.

Gabriel Moran confirms the contemplative need of the young adult, noting that "the special test in our era for this age of life is a growing understanding of non-violence. . . .The realization of a life of nonviolence depends on being tolerant of others views and being willing to learn from enemies."[62] Here are all the components of the contemplative way: nonviolence emerging from the acknowledgement that all beings are interconnected (that they "inter-are" in a neologism recommended by Nhat Hanh[63]); tolerance of other views coming from the realization that truth is not a "block of matter"; above all, learning from enemies, the gift of a spirit which has transcended "comparing, measuring, discriminating, and reacting with attachment and aversion."

Respected during their time as "camels" (childhood), encouraged to cultivate a mindful, silent, and calm inner self even during their time as "lions," we may hope that children, youth, and young adults will achieve that "childhood" of which Nietzsche speaks and which, oddly enough, is so like contemplative being:

> But say, my brothers, what can the child do that even the lion could not do? Why must the preying lion still become a child? The child is innocence and forgetting, a new beginning, a game, a self-propelled wheel, a first move-

ment, a sacred "Yes." For the game of creation, my brothers, a sacred "Yes" is needed: the spirit now wills his own will, and he who had been lost to the world now conquers his own world.

Of three metamorphoses of the spirit I have told you: how the spirit became a camel; and the camel, a lion; and the lion, finally, a child.[64]

PEACEFUL FAMILIES, SACRED DWELLINGS

A rich source of imagery and practice for creating the contemplative family can be found in the work of Kathleen and James McGinnis through the Institute for Peace and Justice in St. Louis, Missouri, in both editions of the wonderful book *Parenting for Peace and Justice*, and in their many lectures and published essays. They have laid out rich images and highly specific processes for promoting the growth of peaceful, nonviolent, receptive, and reflective people within families.

Their fine essay published in 1988 in the journal *Religious Education* is typical: " 'Peace-ing it Together': Family Religious Education for Peace."[65] In the essay, the McGinnises identity five elemental values to be cultivated in family life in such a way that they function as living, dynamic, and habitual qualities of the interior lives of persons within the family as well as within relations among family members and beyond. These values are:

1) self-esteem and affirmation
2) cooperation
3) nonviolent conflict resolution
4) family meetings
5) reconciliation

These are like Annie Dillard's pennies: it is dire poverty indeed, Dillard tells us, if we have grown so jaded that we will not stoop to pick up a penny. In the same way, if we cannot rise to the level of simplicity at which these mechanisms for peaceful family life take on for us a concreteness and urgency, we may be lost. The peaceful family—the sacred dwelling—is one which nourishes self-esteem and affirmation over shame at failed duties, cooperation over competition, nonviolent conflict resolution over corrosive exercise of dominative authority, family meetings over sullen silences, reconciliation over grudges.

To work at the creation of such families is a function of prayerfulness—of contemplative being. The McGinnises associate virtually all of the richness of their vision of peaceful family life with experiences of gratitude, the elemental religious experience, and the persistent contemplative state of consciousness:

> Present, silent, prayerful before the beauty of creation, we all grow in awareness that it is a gift, a gift from God who loves us personally and intensely, and who calls us to care for and share this gift. . . . Present, silent, prayerful before the beauty of creation, we all grow in awareness that we are all one, that all is connected. Returning to Chief Seattle, . . . "This we know. All things are connected, like the blood that unites one family. All things are connected. . . ." Present, silent, prayerful before the beauty of creation, we all grow in our awareness that we are one with future generations, that we have a responsibility to care for the earth and use its resources in such a way that future generations can enjoy them too.[66]

The ecological references are not "stuck in" as another issue. Respect for all creation, a sense of stewardship, is contemplative being. There can be no peaceful family or sacred dwelling which is rabidly and violently consumptive, mindless of the earth. A Zen Buddhist story tells of a young monk traveling far, undergoing many hardships in order to reach a wise man whom he will ask to serve as his master in seeking enlightenment, a man whose wisdom and suitability as guide has been recommended to the young monk by many. But the monk is saddened and discouraged, for upon reaching the isolated camp of the alleged wise man, he sees a piece of lettuce discarded and floating in the stream in front of the camp. The frustrated pilgrim turns away: a wise man would not waste a piece of lettuce; the young monk has been misinformed, no wise man is in residence. Suddenly, the old man bounds from his hut, jumps in the icy stream and wades away in pursuit of the piece of lettuce. The young monk stays; he knows he has not been misinformed.

Maria Harris makes a similar connection between the peaceful family and a reverence for creation in her discussion of the element of family life that she calls "receptivity":

> [Receptivity] implies the readiness to listen to the entire creation addressing us, and ultimately to the Creator Spirit reaching out to be present to us. It is a reminder that before we respond to creation, we first must listen to it and hear it. . . . Receptivity means bringing our contemplative powers to bear on whatever reality lies before us.[67]

In this context, the words of the Buddhist priest Sunyana Graef quoted earlier bear repeating:

> The goal of Buddhist ecology . . . is a life of simplicity, conservation and self-restraint. . .actualized and expressed through the deeds of one's daily life. Such mundane chores as taking out the garbage [and recycling it], cooking a meal, cleaning a toilet and working in the garden are all occasions for cultivation of spiritual awareness.[68]

Many of the themes in this chapter are discussed by Wendy Wright in *Sacred Dwellings: A Spirituality of Family Life*. Wright's book has a power in it that rests in the sincerity and intensity of the personal longing for holiness within family life that the author expresses with candor, as well as in the vividness of her metaphors for holy life within the family. Consider, first, the longing which is expressed:

> I have always wanted to be peaceful within my family. I am not capable of that much of the time. Especially after the birth of my third child, I felt that all the neat ways I

had of coping with my life fell apart. I've always been high strung but suddenly it was all beyond me and I found myself screaming at people a lot and being constantly irritated at my older children who never seemed to stay in line. I felt like a failure. And what was worse, I felt guilty about not being able to hold it all together.

In fact, it was sort of cathartic to have to admit that I couldn't do everything, that I really *needed* God, that I wanted to be peacemaker, but was incapable of being so.[69]

Among the most powerful metaphors which Wright employs to point to the concrete qualities that must "emerge organically" in family spirituality are "nakedness" and "nudity," discussed in the context of intimacy within family.[70] Nakedness is being "vulnerable and transparent"; nudity is a "state of self-consciousness that sees itself as seen." (Earlier, I discussed suspension of self-consciousness as a work of contemplation.) Wright equates "Being a Real Mother" with the "spiritual instruction . . . [of] attentiveness." "Pregnancy" is employed, both literally and metaphorically, as "a time of waiting, . . . the contemplative practice . . . of listening."

In an especially creative sequence, Wright reconsiders the traditional "evangelical counsels," the vows of poverty, chastity and obedience. Poverty is associated with family simplicity, obedience with prophetic justice. The treatment of chastity, however, is particularly arresting. Associating chastity in family life with integrity, Wright invites us to consider it the power to resist being "defined by the cacophony of the 'family ego' or confused by the din of cultural noise."[71]

The final chapter of Sacred Dwellings is entitled "The Is-Ness of Things." It deals, as we might suspect of any thoughtful study of holiness in family, with silence and gratefulness.

The treatment of silence in family life is evocative but idealized. The book ends, however, with a true story about gratitude. Wright recounts a bitter, soul-wrenching and violent family quarrel in which she and her eldest daughter are—or seem to be—the principals:

> Where *was* God in all this? What kind of cosmic joke was this family life? Why didn't anyone *help* me? On and on the relentless thoughts went. . . . Then somehow my mind strayed to a time . . . when I heard a lecture on the religious thought of the Danish philosopher Søren Kierkegaard . . . [who] had written a commentary on the biblical phrase, "In all things, give thanks." In it he describes giving thanks as a formative act, something enjoined on all Christians not because events naturally elicit from us a spirit of gratitude, but because the act of giving thanks itself changed us and our perception. "In all things give thanks." Impossible, I thought, still reeling from the onslaught. . . . Then I heard myself say, somewhat ironically, "Thanks God! Thanks bunches. This is real great." Then I tried it again, dropping the irony and struggling to find the simple place within which at least the words could be uttered. "Thank you" I said flatly. Then again, "Thank you. . . . ." slowly my fixation on my own exhaustion and anger began to give way. "Thank you," I said. And I felt my heart begin to melt. "Thank you for each of them. Thank you for our aliveness. For our here-ness, for the capacity to cry, to scream, to get angry, for the whole thing. For life, for our silly, petty struggles. For the squirming, impossible mess of it all. Yes, genuinely, thank you." And a tender, compassionate love for the is-ness of it all flooded into my heart. All of it. Somehow all deeply blessed. Thank you.[72]

The responsibility of the religious community to promote peaceful families and sacred dwellings is threefold according to Gabriel Moran: to affirm the gift of ordinary family life, resist violence against families, and help families situate themselves within greater communities:

> Religious education is a clear-eyed affirmation of the ordinary, finite family in relation to something greater than the family. One definition of religious education could be: It is whatever affirms the family while at the same time reminding the family that it is not the final community

. . . .Whatever in the environment destroys the family
should be resisted. . . . Negate what negates. . . . Our
society tends to isolate families . . . and to make cooperation difficult. Anything that creates cooperation between
and among families (a neighborhood skill bank, child care
exchange) can without the slightest inflation of the term
be called religious education.[73]

We want to help family members grow as contemplative
beings. The peacefulness of the family and the sacredness of
the dwelling are linked to the contemplative power to invest
each moment and every event with simple significance. Put
another way, the holy family is one which practices the
"experience of the sacrament of the routine":

It is when a person has given assent to this truth [the
sacredness of the routine] but still day after day goes by
and all that he or she does seems just as mundane as ever.
The alarm goes off in the pale light of morning and
another day of work lies ahead. The dishes are piled by
the sink, to be washed once again. The child cries and the
telephone rings, the floor must be washed. Where, one
asks, is the sacredness in any of this? This is where the
discipline of the sacrament of the routine is revealed.[74]

Chapter Six

"Grace Moment by Moment": Practice for Contemplative Being

It remains to speak with some concreteness about practices that help promote contemplative being. In every circumstance the goal of religious educational practice for contemplative formation is to assist those with whom we work to be more responsive to *grace*, for to live life graciously is to live, in Karl Rahner's words, in "the infinity and victory which is God":

> This grace is not a particular phenomenon occurring parallel to the rest of human life but simply the ultimate depth of everything the spiritual creature does. When he realizes himself—when he laughs and cries, accepts responsibility, loves, lives, dies, stands up for truth, breaks out of preoccupation with self to help the neighbor, hopes against hope, cheerfully refuses to be embittered by the stupidity of daily life, keeps silent not so that evil festers in his heart but so that it dies there—when in a word, man lives as he would like to live, in opposition to his selfishness and to the despair that always assails him. This is where grace occurs, because all this leads man into the infinity and victory which is God.[1]

When one lives more responsively to grace, one becomes ever more *grateful*. To be grateful is to pray without ceasing, to "be prayer." Rabbi Heschel says of prayer and gratitude:

> To pray is to regain a sense of the mystery that animates all beings, the divine margin in all attainment. Prayer is

our humble answer to the inconceivable surprise of living. It is all we can offer in return for the mystery by which we live. Who is worthy to be present at the constant unfolding of time? Amidst the meditation of mountains, the humility of flowers—wiser than all alphabets—clouds that die constantly for the sake of God's glory, we are hating, hunting and hurting. Suddenly we feel ashamed of our clashes and complaints in the face of the tacit glory of nature. It is so embarrassing to live! How strange we are in the world, and how presumptuous our doings! Only one response can maintain us: gratefulness for witnessing the wonder, for the gift of our unearned right to serve, to adore, to fulfill. It is gratefulness which makes the soul great.[2]

The practice with which this chapter is concerned is "instructional," offering specific techniques or methods for "schooling" persons in both the desire for meditation and contemplative being and how to practice achieving these ends. If the reader is sympathetic with the ideas expressed in chapters 2 and 3, she or he will not be surprised to find that the content of this chapter is referred to as "instruction" rather than "education." What is contained here is of course intended to be educational. But this series of principles followed by five exercises on meditative and contemplative practice are "schoolteaching" initiatives, a particular expression of "formal education." They are designed to take place within a formal, pastoral educational setting such as a parish church.

I have wanted from the beginning of this enterprise to hold myself to the discipline of articulating specific pastoral initiatives and instructional techniques despite a deep prejudice, discussed from several vantage points in chapter 2, that when it comes to the competence of professional religious educators "good trees bear good fruit," and nothing else need be said. By this I mean that professional parish and congregational religious educators need to "be" a certain way (or be "on" a certain way), need to perceive those with whom they work in a certain way and need to possess—or be possessed by—certain elemental ideas and convictions about the work in which they are engaged. Then all else will, forgive the cliché, "fall into place."

Professional parish or congregational religious educators need to be contemplative; they need to honor the revelations, joys, and sorrows in the ordinary lives of those with whom they work. They need to believe passionately that religious education in the church is preeminently about helping people live faithful, truthful, nonviolent lives (and only secondarily about regularity of creed, code, and cult).

When religious educators are this way, respond to those with whom they work this way, and cherish and advance these beliefs, they are free to practice with simple attention—mindfulness. Then, as the end of a book on religious education draws near, its author can say to them with confidence:

> All that we should do is just do something as it comes. *Do* something! Whatever it is, we should do it, even if it is not-doing something. We should live in this moment. . . . Doing something is expressing our own nature. We do not exist for the sake of something else.[3]

The exercises in contemplative being that follow are framed with a Catholic parish setting in mind. Examples may suggest a predominantly middle-class membership in such a parish. I am very far, however, from considering such a setting, or Catholics of such social and economic characteristics, to be privileged expressions of Catholic or broadly Christian life.

PRINCIPLES FOR PRACTICE
Attracting People to "Exercises in Contemplative Being"

It takes a good deal of practical wisdom to attract people who define themselves as "busy people" to an educational program designed to teach them how to sit still. Fortunately, parish religious educators are often practically wise, familiar with some of the real patterns of people's lives and the pressures which are allowed in some ways to define those patterns. "Buttons have to be pushed"; rhetoric (in the original sense of persuasive language) must be framed to make such programs attractive. Special times, tasks, or experiences can serve as "hooks" in this regard. Here are twelve such circumstances for attracting people to "Exercises in Contemplative Being":

1. *Job/Work*: Exercises in Contemplative Being have to be associated directly, dramatically and forcefully with the joys and sorrows of the workplace outside the home. After every program of three, four, or five or more sessions has ended, parish leadership might think about beginning a new one designed to invite members of the religious community to talk about their work—the pressures, the anxieties, the challenges, and joys—and to link competence in the meditative practice to the desire to survive, resist, or reject the scattering of the soul through difficulties at work.

2. *Parenthood*: New parents, parents of several children, parents stretched by the dispersing effects of a rush of activity associated with many children, parents who are a bit disappointed in the way they cope, how they displace anger on children, especially parents of adolescents, should be invited, in the light of these responsibilities and perceived needs, to sit down (literally and figuratively) and engage in Exercises in Contemplative Being.

3. *Passage: from High School and* 4. *Passage: from College:* Contemplative retreats just prior to high school and college graduation should be promoted with wry humor. The possibilities of young women and men getting "eaten up" in the world or in college might be exploited in the effort to attract teenagers and young adults to Exercises in Contemplative Being. An especially impressive framework for such retreats is provided by Patricia Tracey and her colleagues at Christian Brothers Academy in Lincroft, New Jersey. The senior retreat program at this school is a beautifully sculptured mix of emphases on contemplative and medita-

tive being, revelations in nature and specific christological themes. The framework for this exercise in contemplative being was published in the October, 1991 issue of *Professional Approaches For Christian Educators,* volume 21.

5. *Confirmation:* When confirmation serves as the free, honest culmination of the *beginnings* of educational formation of young adults, Exercises in Contemplative Being can be especially beneficial. Where Eastern, for example Buddhist, elements of the meditative life are studied and practiced alongside the Christian, such a feature of preparation for confirmation can take advantage of the intrinsically curious nature of the "foreign" element. The quality of thoughtfulness ("being delivered to oneself as a subject") that a meditative component of confirmation catechesis provides can also help teenagers and young adults to be reflective about the element of will or desire in this extended sacramental moment, whether they, in fact, wish to engage in this sacramental act or whether it is a conventional, routinized act with potential for promoting cynicism and a sense of the vacuity of religious ritual. In this regard, Michael Warren's earnest suggestion in *Faith, Culture and the Worshipping Community* that many young adults need a "confirmation annulment" is worth noting.

6. *RCIA:* The emphasis on prayerfulness that is already a stock-in-trade of most RCIA programs can be enhanced and brought to fullness by inclusion of a contemplative dimension.

7. *Retirement:* Any reasonably large congregation will have people in their middle or later middle years who may be attracted to Exercises in Contemplative Being framed as an opportunity to consider what life's next great transition may bring. Such individuals would join others on the verge of retirement whose need for psychic preparation (without dwelling too far in the future) for this new way of being attracts them to the Exercises.

8. *Turning 30, 40, 50, 60, 70 . . . :* I think of this "hook" as a "natural." Again, a critical mass of members of a local reli-

gious community can presumably always be found who are turning 30, 40, 50, and so on. Concerns raised by the age-heterogeneity of those who might come out for Exercises in Contemplative Being targeted in this fashion should be off-set by the potential for rich conversation across generations.

9. Homemakers: For every homemaker who feels chal-lenged, alert and growing, there is another woman (and an increasing number of men) who do not experience working in the home or the role of homemaker as vital and vitalizing. This book has dealt with the rapture of investing ordinary work with deep meaning, performing one's work with attention, simplicity, and gratitude. But domestic work is not a revelatory experience giving rise to thanksgiving for many men and women who are homemakers. In addition to the social and intellectual stimulation and support that local religious communities should provide homemakers, Exer-cises in Contemplative Being might be promoted with this population precisely because the Exercises help us see the beauty and the strength of ordinary work.

10. Seasons: The Advent theme of waiting, with it con-notation of paying attention, being alert, not forgetting that each moment is a masterpiece or can be, affords an oppor-tunity to attract members of the community to a discipline of creative and peaceful waiting.

Enhanced meaning can also be ascribed to repentance, *teshuvah*—turning around—when "Lenten spirituality" em-bodies Exercises in Contemplative Being. This is the expres-sion of the ultimate experience of a "changed heart": contemplation as liberation from irritation, anger, frustration, dispersion, scatteredness, anxiety, and fear—so much of it rooted in the delusional thinking which comes from ego-centeredness. Lent should be "publicized" as the time to get our "stuff" together through Exercises in Contemplative Being.

11. Death: I admit my ignorance about the pattern of bereavement ministry which, thankfully, has become a com-mon feature of the formal but responsive and experimental pastoral educational programming of many congregations. In both Christian and Buddhist wisdom and practice the participation of all being in a overarching and embracing Reality, and thus the imperishability of all being, constitutes the heart of the teaching, the purpose of practice. It is inconceivable that presence to those who have suffered the loss of loved ones would not entail the gentle invitation to learn, practice, and steadily develop a way of life illuminated by the traditions of meditation.

12. *Sorrow*: This is a contrived and redundant category, but one on which it is necessary to focus. During their conversations on Public Broadcasting, Bill Moyers asked Joseph Campbell whether, having established a discipline that allowed one to find the "center" and "follow your bliss," one would then change the world. Campbell responded: "The world is a wasteland. . . . Change yourself." Shakyamuni Buddha put it even more directly 2500 years ago: "All life is suffering." Joy and sorrow do not have parity as occasions for encouraging practice of contemplative being. More often than not—much more often than not—the sorrowful experience, despite its power to destroy, may be the occasion for experiencing the grace to turn to the practice of contemplative being. Specific suffering of specific people is not the springboard for programming the Exercises in Contemplative Being. But if the religious educators are on the way themselves, they may be quite literally "instruments of peace." Having awakened, they practice being on this path. Because of their discipline of life, they are present to the suffering of others and invite them to begin, or begin again, the journey to overcome suffering through this practice of peace—contemplative practice.

Flexibility in the Exercises in Contemplative Being

This principle should "go without saying," yet I want to emphasize a specific aspect of flexible use of these Exercises. The Exercises are highly *participatory*, and *discursive elements* should be introduced within the broadly participatory character of these exercises whenever the expressed desires of participants and/or the intuitions of the persons conducting the Exercises warrant. It is to be hoped that the text of this book itself provides a good deal of content for *presentation and reflective conversation* that can be thoughtfully and appropriately interpolated into the sequence of activities in each Exercise. When working with professional or amateur catechists, young adults, or groups formed around questions of work or family life, it may be appropriate to "teach" parts of the content of this book, supplemented greatly by other texts. Another interpolation of content may be to discuss *qualities* of meditative practice and contemplative being, such as silence or gratefulness or paying attention.

I belabor the point about flexibility because of my experience of many years of seeing religious educators stick slavishly to either a predominantly discursive or a predominantly participatory style, with little recourse to the desires of those with whom they are working. The classical blind spot is that "my words," "my lecture" is revelatory; who could fail to be interested, indeed moved! A more modern blind spot has been to banish the presentation in favor of the presumed vividness of vicarious—or contrived—experiences embodied in creative "participatory games." In choosing between content, presented and discussed, and participatory activities, let balance and responsiveness to those engaged in the Exercises in Contemplative Being be the rule.

Employ Eastern and Western Ideas and Practices

This principle may seem a bit odd. An implicit but dominant premise of this work is that the richness of Christian, Jewish, and Eastern, especially Buddhist, ideas and practices need to be integrated and presented in these exercises. I am concerned, however, that professional religious educators, even those who feel comfortable with these crosscultural insights, may be tempted to drop them, not out of lack of appreciation or fear but because they feel participants will be confused or bemused by programs of "spiritual formation" that weld Buddhist and Christian insight together. Resist this assumption! Say to yourself and to those with whom you work what Abbot Thomas Keating has said of the providential meeting of visions of interiority of world religions: "The contemplative dimension of life, present in all the great religions, is the common heart of the world. There the human family is already one."[4]

It may be helpful to frame Exercises in Contemplative Being alongside the recent and rich popularization of apophatic spirituality called "centering prayer" and to share the history of this movement and its association with Cisterians—Merton, Keating, and Basil Pennington. I should not like to see technique reduced to Pennington's three simple rules for centering prayer. However, their very simplicity as well as their association with Christian sources recommend these techniques:

> Rule One: At the beginning of the prayer we take a minute or two to quiet down and then move in faith to God dwelling in our depths; and at the end of the prayer we take several minutes to come back, mentally praying the Our Father. . . .

> Rule Two: After resting for a bit in the center in faith-full love, we take up a single, simple word that expresses this response and begin to let it repeat itself within. . . .

> Rule Three: Whenever in the course of the prayer we become aware of anything else, we simply gently return to the prayer word."[5]

Along the same lines, Christian and Hebrew scripture can be employed extensively in the Exercises to follow. Though I make only modest reference to Christian scripture, I consider the effort to parallel Buddhist and Christian insight a powerful tool. For example, Buddhism counsels us to "let go" of clinging through the practice of emptiness; Jesus of Nazareth proclaims that those who try to save their lives will lose them; those who lose—let go of—their lives will save them. To encourage the reader who may use these Exercises, I have appended a brief synopsis of select themes in Matthew's Gospel correlated with teachings about liberation within Mahayana Buddhism. Matthew was chosen arbitrarily; religious educators who are or who become knowledgeable and appreciative of Eastern insight may wish to study other elements of Christian scripture and develop their own parallels. Paul's theology of the "mystical body" and of "new being" in Christ Jesus, as well as his evocation of Spirit and suffering in Romans, are especially rich areas for integration with Eastern ideas.

Orthodoxy: Breath and Posture;
All Else is Experimentation

Meditative or contemplative practice, prayerfulness, centering prayer—all these by whatever name will engage participants in a variety of activities: sitting cross-legged, or in some cases in the full- or semi-lotus position, lying down, walking gently, sitting in a chair, tucking their calves under a stool and resting their backsides on a cushion atop the stool. Participants may repeat a word over and over to the pattern of their breath or, in the same rhythm, "speak" *gathas*, or sayings, or prayers long or short with the voice of their inner life. Or the counting of breaths, a warm-up exercise ordinarily, may give way to gentle efforts to achieve complete interior silence. At other times it may be desirable to breathe/meditate through a particularly irritating "wave" of the mind, a preoccupation or distraction that will not leave consciousness until it has been treated with sufficient love and kindness. Sometimes all will be still in the external environment and no stimulus for ear or eye available. At other times, a candle may be lit and placed in the center of a group of persons engaged in meditation and appropriate music played gently in the background.

The point is this: virtually every aspect of the physical and external as well as the interior environment of meditative practice for contemplative being is subject to *experimentation*. Those conducting exercises should regularly remind participants that there is no single mode of practice, uniform in all detail, to which they must measure up.

Two aspects of practice are, however, not subject to negotiation: breath and posture. Efforts should be made at the very beginning of Exercises in Contemplative Being to communicate the essential place of breathing pattern in meditative practice. The "true men [and women] of Tao [or the "new being" in Christ Jesus] breathe from their ankles not from their stomach," as Chuang Tsu said. The insight we experience on the brink of engaging in a challenging and anxious enterprise ("just breathe deeply and go get 'um") and more systematically practiced in natural child birthclasses is elevated to unshakable and certain "doctrine" in meditative practice.

It is only a little less crucial that participants be encouraged to begin now, in meditative practice and moment by moment every day, to sit, stand, and walk in a straight-backed position. Ask participants to trust you at the beginning; the ineffable relationship between being "collected" and having a straight back and a steady, gentle, rhythmic, and deep breathing pattern will become manifest.

EXERCISES IN CONTEMPLATIVE BEING
Exercise 1: "Beginner's Mind"

I am suggesting more "script" for presentation and discussion in this first exercise than I will for exercises 2 through 5. Subsequent exercises deal with the "qualities" of contemplative being discussed throughout the text of this book. Those conducting Exercises in Contemplative Being may wish to consult portions of the book in which these qualities are examined as an aid in constructing the "text" for introducing and discussing various of these qualities.

DISCURSIVE INTRODUCTION

If you were given a choice between being "together" or torn into hundreds of pieces; "collected" or scattered all about; empty of various interior "toxic wastes" like the Seven Deadly Sins or filled with such waste material; open moment by moment and alert to possibilities or "tied up in a knot," not even noticing in any sustained or appreciative way what is in fact going on right around you: if you could choose to be peaceful rather than "strung out," which would you choose?

The exercises in which we will engage tonight are exercises designed to deepen our capacity for *human excellence.* They are about learning to be at peace, or, as one Zen master frames it, actually "being peace." They offer a choice between existing more or less all the time in a state of irritation, anxiety, fear, frustration, anger, jealousy, and envy, or just "being peace," being contemplative or meditative.

For some, mediative practice is solely a physical discipline for getting collected after they have been scattered; they do not expect to meet anyone other than themselves in the quieted space that they enter when they practice with real athletic enterprise to become calm and interiorly silent. And that reflective meeting with oneself is highly beneficial.

For others—and they would more likely call the exercise "contemplation" or prayer—there is an expectation that God, the "Silent Infinite" within us and yet encompassing us, is encountered in the silence of meditation.

EXPLANATION OF METHOD

Tonight we are going to practice meditative or contemplative being. If you catch a whisper of the life-giving force (in the sense of the book of Deuteronomy's call to resist death and choose life) . . . if you catch a whisper of the life-giving force or power of just sitting still, quietly doing nothing, breathing in and breathing out . . . it will become like oxygen. You will stop playing the game called "I'm a busy person . . . I have no time." You will "have" time rather than, as the Zen Masters say, time "having" you. The one or two sustained times of sitting quietly that you engage in each day, especially early in the morning, will serve as a power source; you will then have small "bites" of peace and calm and "centeredness" between phone calls, waiting on lines, stopped in traffic jams and, more importantly, just as you are about to say something unkind to a loved one, or anyone. If you keep to your practice you will be able to induce these smaller "bites" more easily as time goes by.

Sitting in a circle on pillows on the floor or on chairs, with backs straight and hands folded peacefully in laps or, finally, seated with calves tucked under a stool and backside resting on a pillow on stop of the stool, participants are introduced to the initiatory process of counting their breaths: count one as you inhale, and one as you exhale. Continue slowly to the count of ten, perhaps also concentrating on the tip of your nose. The Zen *gatha* (saying) composed by Nhat Hanh may be recited by the person conducting the exercise and the participants invited to "say" this *gatha* within themselves to the rhythm of their breathing: "Breathing in I calm my body/breathing out I smile. Dwelling in the present moment/I know this is a wonderful moment." Music is played quietly in the background. Examples of suitable music that I have used with groups engaged in meditative practice include: "Music for Zen Meditation" by Tony Scott, Shinichi Yuize, and Hozan Yamamoto (Polygram Records); "Eastern Peace" by Steven Halpern (Halpern Sounds); or any Greogorian chant.

At the ten minute point, a bell is gently "invited to ring" (a term prefered by Zen masters), and the conductor of the exercise speaks the following excerpt from Nhat Hanh's commentary on the "Sutra on the Full Awareness of Breathing":

The bell of mindfulness is the voice of the Buddha [or of Christ] calling us back to ourselves. We should respect this sound, stop thinking and talking and return to ourselves with breathing and a smile.

Participants continue to sit in quiet meditation, the music having been turned off but the bell gently struck every forty-five seconds or so for the next ten minutes.

At the twenty minute point, the person conducting the exercises reads the following saying, again of Nhat Hanh, interspersing the "ringing" of the bell as indicated:

Do not lose yourself in dispersion and in your surroundings. [bell intonation]
Learn to practice breathing in order to regain compose of mind and body [bell intonation]
to regain mindfulness [bell intonation]
[pause]
and to develop concentration and understanding. [bell intonation]

Allow up to another five minutes of silent seated meditation, gauging the amount of time by when some movement, throat clearing, or other signs of distraction occur. Bring this first seated meditation to a conclusion by quietly saying: "Hold your being secure and quiet. / Keep your life collected in its own center. / Do not allow your thoughts to be disturbed by anything"; and, after another thirty seconds or so, "Come Holy Spirit / Come Holy Spirit."

This is a moderately "busy" meditation session in deference to those participants who may need these multiple promptings to regain composure in meditation and come back from "mind waves," or distractions. Those conducting the sessions need to be especially attentive to the suitability of assisting quiet sitting with these contrivances. As participants grow in their ability to attain calm relatively speedily, they may find any, all or some of these techniques—music, bells, sayings—distracting rather than helpful.

CONCLUDING ACTIVITIES

1. There should be time for conversation in which participants express their experience in this first meditation session.

2. Those conducting the session should find a time in this final phase to emphasize the need to treat "mind waves" with nonviolence, gently turning them around and resuming centered calm by resuming the original breathing exercise. A second point that should be made is that if painful distractions inhabit our interiority, we may need to "invite" them to remain, and breathe through a steady contemplation of the source of the problem in hope that in such a state of calm the pain, fear, and anxiety can be encountered with equanimity.

3. In a conversational conclusion to this first exercise there should be a rehashing of the centrality of the spiritual and physical discipline of breathing gently and rhythmically. It may be that the seemingly miraculous relationship between calm, presence, readiness, silence, equanimity—in short, mindfulness—and breathing pattern can be "oversold." But if the participants seem amenable, those conducting this exercise might in fact reproduce (with permission) the sixteen parts of the *Anapansatti sutra*, the "Sutra on the Full Awareness of Breathing," from the book *Breath: You Are Alive* by Thich Nhat Hanh (Parallax Press, Berkeley, California). Nhat Hanh's commentary on this ancient text of Shakyamuni Buddha is a spiritual classic. Four of the final five exercises in the part of the sutra dealing with full awareness of breathing may give the reader a sense of their power. Subject to judgments about the openness of the participants to insight from this "foreign" source, a whole exercise can profitably be given over to this text:

12. I am breathing in and liberating my mind. I am breathing out and liberating my mind. He practices like this.
13. I am breathing in and observing the impermanent

nature of all dharmas [all phenomenon, impermanent in their present form but imperishable because, as water is *in* each wave life is *in* and remains in each existing reality]. I am breathing out and observing the impermanent nature of all dharmas. He practices like this. . . . 15. I am breathing in and contemplating liberation. I am breathing out and contemplating liberation. . . . 16. I am breathing in and contemplating letting go. I am breathing out and contemplating letting go. He practices like this.[6]

If time allows and those conducting the exercise think that participants are open to further discursive elements, a brief discussion of the "qualities" of contemplative being and fruits of meditative practice on which subsequent exercises will focus may be serve as the concluding portion of Exercise 1.

If you named this exercise "Beginner's Mind" as I have, you may want to conclude by explaining that the beginner's mind is the pure, simple, uncluttered mind. In this context, "mind" means all of me, the five Skandhas: body or form, feeling, objects of the mind, perceptions, and consciousness. Quote from the first page of Shunryu Suzuki's classic *Zen Mind Beginner's Mind,* where he says that everything is possible for those with beginner's mind; their minds are not a block of stuff. It is the experts for whom little is possible; their minds are already full.

Be prepared for some concern to be expressed by one or more participants over the blending of Eastern, especially Buddhist, and Christian "spiritualities." Abbot Keating's observation quoted above may be helpful. The regard expressed for Zen by Thomas Merton cited in chapter 1 may also be noted to reassure participants who consider this effort at blending inappropriate.

Exercise 2: Silent Encounter

INTRODUCTION

Introductory remarks should simply and briefly point to silence as a quality of contemplative being available through meditative practice to the person who is willing to practice. Meister Eckhart's saying that "nothing in all creation is so like God as silence" might be tied to St. Paul's proclamation in Acts that "in God we live and move and have our being." That God is silence and we are in God suggests that our legacy is to dwell always in silence, refreshing silence even in the midst of busyness, even sorrow.

MINI-MEDITATION

Exercises 2 through 5 conclude with a substantial meditation period. They should begin with a two to three minute meditation period. I suggest the following pattern:

1. Participants are invited to resume the body position they took last week or experiment with another one; those who might have been scared off by sitting on a meditation pillow on the floor in cross-legged position, for example, might try it tonight.

2. Count breaths for a minute.

3. In one's interior self "say" one or two brief Christian and Buddhist *gathas*: "Come Holy Spirit"; "Come Lord Jesus"; "In God, we live and move and have our breathing"; "Hold your being secure and quiet/Keep your life collected in its own center/Do not allow anything to disturb your thoughts"; or "Breathing in I calm my body, breathing out I smile/Dwelling in the present moment/I know this is a wonderful moment."

4. Allow another two or three minutes of quiet meditation and then invite participants to "come out of it."

EXPLANATION OF METHOD

1. Create five minutes, five full minutes, of *noise*. The noise should be shrill, alternating, and coming from several sources, with each kind of noise sustained for at least thirty seconds. Don't overdo it, but don't "underdo" it. Create a lot of noise from a variety of sources.

2. Stop noise abruptly without explanation and provide two full minutes of quiet, inviting the bell to ring four times at thirty second intervals.

3. Sponsor a brief discussion of the contrast, with obvious questions such as "Which did you prefer?" Blaise Pascal said, "All mankind's misery comes from this, that they are unable to be alone in a little room." (You may also wish to quote Merton's thoughts about being in the woods, in the cabin, in the rain not doing or having anything.)

4. Ask and promote conversation about whether Pascal's statement is true of us: Can we be alone, quietly in a room? Ask participants to think about the past week: what was the wakeful time of the longest sustained silence? Was it pleasurable or laborious, chosen or enforced? Where did it occur?

5. Ask participants during the coming week to be in a "room" alone, apart from their periods of seated meditation. Discuss when they might do it and where, what they will need to arrange in order to do it. Make it clear that this is not to be quite the same as seated meditation, which we hope they are practicing once or twice every day. They should do something with this time; they should do it deliberately, calmly, with grace, seeking gently to derive more pleasure from the doing than might ordinarily be the case. Perhaps they could arrange to prepare and cook a meal alone without rushing.

MEDITATIVE PRACTICE

Before beginning the twenty to thirty minute seated meditation which concludes this and all subsequent exercise sessions, some discussion of how meditation went during the prior week should be occur. Again, those conducting the exercises need to encourage *experimentation*. And, in this second sustained period of meditation, prudential judgment is needed to decide what balance of silent sitting and music, bell ringing and sayings should occur.

Exercise 3: Awake and Aware

INTRODUCTION

One or at most two of the following ideas derived from
the text of this book might serve to introduce the exercise
session: Nhat Hanh on "Washing the Dishes"; Monica Hellwig on contemplation as "vulnerability," allowing things,
events, people to really happen; Shunryu Suzuki on stopping, observing, thinking clearly even amidst busyness.
Tonight we wish to concentrate on paying attention, just
simply being awake and aware, "being there when we are
there"!

MINI-MEDITATION

As in Exercise 2, or as revised as a result of discussion of
what suits participants best.

EXPLANATION OF METHOD

1. Did you drive here? Did you walk here? How did you
drive or walk? Carefully, thoughtfully, deliberately? Or were
you absent to the activity?

2. How, typically, do you walk, eat, sit down, and
stand up?

3. If the participants are prone to be playful, play it out;
play act sitting, walking, driving a car, and eating in a scattered and dispersed fashion and then in an awake and
aware fashion.

4. Send everyone on a ten minute solitary walk; ask
them to try to be awake during this walk.

5. When participants recongregate, ask them to talk
about what they heard, saw, experienced; of what sounds,
sights and smells they were aware.

6. Ask participants to reflect on the last couple of days;
when were they awake and aware, when absent and dis-
tracted and, above all, *with whom.* Lead the conversation to
a discussion of absence to others and introduce the quality
of contemplative being, presence. Here, I recommend quot-

ing Nhat Hanh's discussion of being bound to anxieties and fears and anger rooted in being pulled back into the past and drawn forward into the future, and his proposal that to experience the joy running like sap through every existing reality we must think of our lives as taking knots out of thread, something which requires calm and takes time. (These observations are discussed in chapter 1.) Conclude by suggesting that the brokenness of many relations is a function of lack of presence; that we lack presence because we are filled with toxic wastes in the form of fears and resentments that drive us out of the present back to the past or into the future. Meditation empties us (perhaps read the kenotic hymn in Philippians 2 in which Christ is depicted as emptying himself) and promotes the equanimity ("being peace") that allows us to live as Jesus taught. The "lilies of the field" portion of the Sermon on the Mount discourse from the Gospel of Matthew, chapter 6, can serve as a conclusion as well as a springboard to meditative practice.

MEDITATIVE PRACTICE

As in Exercise 2.

Exercise 4: Readiness and Busyness

It's time to shift sequence and type of activities in order to avoid uncreative sameness. No discursive introduction, no mini-meditation.

EXPLANATION OF METHOD

1. Begin with the questions: What is it that you do with style and grace? What comes naturally to you, even if it has taken years of discipline? What comes naturally to you *now*? A particular dish you prepare, meeting new people, speaking in public, a golf swing, how you shake hands or walk, how you garden, how you "work a system" (for example, governmental agencies or their child or children's school situation), writing, calming a child, etc.? Stay with this until

everyone who wishes to speak has unearthed something they do with relative effortlessness, style and grace. Suggest that for some set of reasons, some complex of causes that may not nor need not be fully understood or articulated, in performing that activity they are *ready*, they are present to the task with a "natural simplicity" (Saint Bernard) rooted in being uncluttered, unafraid and—of course—good at it!

2. Try to get everyone to unearth a strength, because you now ask them to root through their minds for a task or recurring circumstance that nearly always finds them befuddled, mildly or greatly anxious just as they are about to perform it, and vaguely or distinctly unhappy with the performance of the task just as it is completed. Often enough examples entail use of telephones, especially speaking to someone's telephone answering machine.

3. Cite Shunryu Suzuki on the smooth, clear way of thinking even when you are caught up in busyness that might make your mind "ragged." Also cite Jesus in Matthew 10:19-21, enjoining his disciples not to be anxious about what they are to say even when they are about to confront their persecutors into whose hands they have been delivered.

4. This may be a good time to consider the strictly pragmatic, functional benefits of meditative calm, especially the effort to develop the habit of practicing multiple "bites," moments interspersed throughout every day, of recollecting oneself, counting breaths, "saying" a *gatha* or prayer within one's interior self, and "being peace."

5. Ask participants to think about the next time they are likely to be placed in the situation of performing the task that induces a certain dread; ask if they are getting a bit anxious even now.

6. Even if you have used the texts before, I recommend slow, expressive reading of Nhat Hanh's saying about "Washing the Dishes" and Jesus' words on the "lilies of the field."

MEDITATIVE PRACTICE

As in prior sessions, with brief discussion of the best interplay of elements.

Exercise 5: Letting Go and Compassion

Again, a variation in sequence of activities is suggested.

MINI-MEDITATION

As in Exercise 2.

EXPLANATION OF METHOD

1. Jesus says that unless you *lose* yourself, you will be lost. All the great Eastern spiritual masters talk about "holding yourself," not being "scattered"; for example, a few weeks ago we quoted Nhat Hanh, "Do not lose yourself in dispersion and in your surroundings." Back to a Christian source, the great thirteenth-century mystic, Meister Eckhart, says that if you do not lose yourself, or as he says let go and stop clinging to things, God cannot be born: "There, where clinging to things ends, God begins to be."

2. So, we have two questions. The first: in our gentle efforts to be contemplative beings are we "in the business" of losing ourselves or holding on to ourselves? (Presumably, conversation will ensue along the line "both according to a certain meaning.") Sunyana Graef's pointed remarks cited in the discussion of ego-centeredness and later in the discussion of emptiness in chapter 3 may be helpful to bring in at some point in the conversation: the self trapped in the narrow world of delusional thinking must be let go of; the true self is then found.

> Delusional thinking devolves from the ego, miring people in greed and jealousy, creating destructive emotions of hatred and anger and leaving a legacy of loneliness and pain. Most people are at the mercy of their bodies and mistaken belief, falling prey to neuroses and addictions in an attempt to palliate their emptiness. . . . It is what we

do not have—self-centeredness, immaturity, greed and anger—that enables us to live a compassionate life full of peace and freedom.

3. The less obvious question to which those conducting this exercise should turn the participants' attention entails the use of the word "self." Introduce a discussion of me, us, each of our "selves," by reading Nhat Hanh's words on a piece of paper:

> If you are a poet you will see clearly that there is a cloud floating in this piece of paper. Without a cloud there will be no water; without water, the tree cannot grow; and without trees, you cannot not have paper. So the cloud is in here. The existence of this page is dependent on the existence of a cloud. Paper and cloud are so close. Let us think of other things, like sunshine. Sunshine is very important because the forest cannot grow without sunshine. So the logger needs sunshine in order to cut the tree, and the tree needs sunshine in order to be a tree. Therefore you can see sunshine in this sheet of paper. And if you look more deeply. . . . with the eyes of those who are awake you see not only the cloud and the sunshine in it, but that everything is here: the wheat that became the bread for the logger to eat, the logger's father, everything is in the sheet of paper.[7]

4. Ask the participants to substitute themselves for the piece of paper and quietly reflect, with paper and pencil in hand, on all the so-called non-self (non-paper) "elements" that really constitute them. Encourage breathing and creativity of reflection by suggesting that they try to think across many categories just as Nhat Hanh has: elements of who and what and when (for time is part of my self), past and present, personal and non-personal, joyful and sorrowful, etc.

5. Invite participants to discuss with one another some—if not all—the elements of self which have come to mind.

6. Ask the participants to consider whether there is such a great difference between the Eastern, especially Buddhist,

notion of *annatta* (literally no soul), that there is no individual reality but only interdependent reality, and the implications of the biblical theology of Christ's mystical body, brought to special ethical significance in Matthew's "endtimes" discourse of Jesus, chapter 25 ("if you did it . . . if you did not do it for one of these the least of my brethren . . .").

7. A fairly substantial conversation might ensue— though this exercise has been pretty wordy—on contemplation and compassion. At least the distortion, to which I made reference in chapter 1, that equates meditation and contemplative with ethical and relational disinterest can be repudiated.

8. Ask participants to share with one another whether their weeks of effort—gentle effort we hope—to engage in meditative practice and be contemplative beings has made them more compassionate, more patient. Has it become increasingly clear in meditation that there is no duality? Perhaps this part of the exercise can conclude with a quotation from Gabriel Moran: "To be morally adult is to know. . . . [that] if we let the choice [all choice, the realm of moral life] flow from the center of our *receptiveness to being* and in resonance with fellow travelers on earth, our actions will have a gentleness that lessens the violence in the world."[8]

MEDITATIVE PRACTICE

As in previous exercises.

Epilogue: Paying Attention

In the final chapter of their book, *The Good Society*, Robert Bellah and his collaborators address the breakdown of participatory democracy in the United States. Though the purpose of "Democracy Means Paying Attention" is different from that of this book, the opening words serve to summarize important elements of this work.

> From the time we were children we were told by our parents and our grammar school teachers to "pay attention!" In more or less preemptory ways we have been receiving the same message ever since. Even though we may have grown inured to this injunction and shrug it off, there are few things in life more important. For paying attention is how we use our psychic energy, and how we use our psychic energy determines the kind of self we are cultivating, the kind of person we are learning to be. When we are giving our full attention to something, when we are really attending, we are calling on all our resources of intelligence, feeling, and moral sensitivity. This can happen at work, at play, in interaction with people we care about. At such moments we are not thinking about ourselves, because we are completely absorbed in what we are doing. Although such moments are enjoyable, we do not seek them out because of pleasure, but because they are things we really want to do in terms of the larger context of our lives. They "make sense." And even though they are moments of minimal self-consciousness and

their purpose is not to maximize pleasure, it is in such moments that we are most likely to be genuinely happy.[1]

Meditative practice leading to contemplative being is a matter of learning to pay attention. In Zen Buddhism, it is mindfulness or presence. The shalom of Judaism, the peace of wholeness, is in part dependent on to what we chose to give our attention. Christian holiness, the faithfulness of which I spoke in the introduction to this book, is a matter of "patient attentiveness." Education, understood as the patterns of relationships that induce faithfulness, is a work of attentiveness. Whether the communities to which we give ourselves and which in turn form us are places in which we wrestle with the meaning of our existence and the moral purposes of our human work depends on the members of the community who are paying attention.

Contemplative beings pay attention to the Source and in doing so become conscious of their own subjectivity. It is this consciousness—really taking possession of our sub-jectivity—that Rahner identifies with truly having being, and Nhat Hanh calls the capacity to resist being slapped about like a bottle by the waves.

In paying attention to the Source the contemplative being is also filled with awe and gratitude for the gifts of ordinary life. Such persons are filled with reverence for other beings, human and nonhuman, and with resistance born of compassion when confronted with beings who are excluded from the gifts of ordinary life.

Religious communities such as the church, too, must pay attention. If it is to be a true community in which real education occurs, the church must pay attention to its essential function of forming contemplatives. Martin Buber knew that apart from this priority religion is inevitably degenerate: "The degeneration of religions means the degeneration of prayer in them: the relational power in them is buried more and more by objecthood."[2]

Writing about paying attention under the rubric mindfulness, Nhat Hanh says that without this ability "we are incapable of actually living one moment of our lives." This is finally what is at stake in cultivating contemplative being: Life lived at a level of peace and compassion. And, as Gustavo Gutiérrez has said, there is no third way between the Deuteronomic choice between life and death. We must choose life!

Appendix

As noted at the beginning of chapter 6, I have surveyed one Gospel as a case in point, in order to identify themes in the teachings of Jesus that correspond in distinct ways with insights of Eastern spirituality, especially Mahayana Buddhism, and more especially the Soto school of Zen Buddhism.

This listing contains citations from the Gospel of Matthew, a brief phrase or clause identifying the substance of the scripture, and an equally brief phrase or clause identifying the corresponding Buddhist idea. As I noted earlier, it is crucial that this listing be taken as *an example* only. Readers inclined to promote the kind of educational program that encourages meditative practice and nurtures contemplative being would do well to survey the whole Christian scripture, and also certain wisdom literature and much of Isaiah, for example, from the Hebrew scripture. They would thereby develop their own rich resource for harmonizing Jewish, Christian, and Buddhist wisdom in education for contemplative formation.

1. Mt. 6:25—Lilies of the field/*Equanimity in the face of suffering, activity with a quality of aimlessness (apranihita)*

2. Mt. 7:2—Do not judge; Mt. 12: 9ff.—The single sheep in the pit; Mt. 18:10ff.—I came to save the lost; Mt. 13:24-30—Weeds growing up with wheat/*It is never very clear what is right and what is wrong, what is for the good, what pro-*

duces evil; it is best to live an enlightened, nonviolent life and leave moralism to others

3. Mt. 8:26, 10:26ff.—Do not be afraid/*Equanimity overcoming suffering*

4. Mt. 27:31—Blind men; Mt. 23—The blind guides[1]/ *Wake up, see*

5. Mt. 10:19-21—Do not be anxious about what to say/*"Being peace," overcoming anxiety, scatteredness*

6. Mt. 10:38ff., 16:24—Find life by losing it/*Letting go*

7. Mt. 11:25ff., 18—Little children make up the kingdom; Mt. 19:13ff.—Revelation to the little ones/*Cultivating utter, interior silence and simplicity*

8. Mt. 11:29—Meek and humble; Mt. 13:31ff.—The mustard seed/*The true man or woman of Tao whose law is within themselves*

9. Mt. 12:31-37—The Spirit and the abundance of the heart/*Dwelling in "Buddha mind" or "Big Mind," speaking, like Bodhidarma, with pure, peaceful assurance*

10. Mt. 13:15ff.—The hard of heart neither see nor hear/*Interior purification and being awake*

11. Mt. 19:16-26—On riches/*Simplicity of lifestyle, Buddhist ecology according to Graef*

12. Mt. 20:1-16—Laborers in the vineyard, the owner's reasons not being understood by the laborers who came in the first hour/*Transcending simple, rationalistic "cause and effect" thinking in favor of paradoxical and intuitive contemplative thinking*[2]

13. Mt. 24:36-42—Watchfulness; Mt. 25:1-13—The ten virgins/*Being awake*

14. Mt. 25:31-46—Endtime discourse, the poor who are helped, the poor who are spurned are Christ/*Tao, "Buddha mind"*[3]

Notes

INTRODUCTION

1. Gabriel Moran, *No Ladder to the Sky: Education and Morality* (San Francisco: Harper and Row, 1987), p. 177.

CHAPTER ONE

1. Thich Nhat Hanh, *Breath, You Are Alive* (Berkeley: Parallax Press, 1988), p. 52.

2. Moshe Idel, *Kabbalah New Perspectives* (New Haven: Yale University Press, 1988). I am indebted to Rabbi Lawrence Kushner for bringing this work to my attention as well as many traditions and sources of an essentially "absorptive" Jewish mysticism of which I was unaware.

3. Thomas Merton, *New Seeds of Contemplation* (Norfolk, Conn.: New Directions, 1961), p. 1.

4. Nhat Hanh, *Breath*, pp. 32f.

5. Quoted in Dick Westley, *Morality and Its Beyond* (Mystic, Conn.: Twenty-Third Publications, 1984).

6. Sunyana Graef, "A Hair in Vast Space: Teaching and Learning in Zen," *Religious Education*, Volume 84, Number 2 (Spring, 1989), p. 181.

7. Merton, *New Seeds*, p. 1.

8. Abraham J. Heschel in Samuel H. Dresner (ed.), *I Asked for Wonder* (New York: Crossroad, 1991), p. 20.

9. Thomas Merton, *Mystics and Zen Masters* (New York: Farrar, Strauss and Giroux, 1967), p. 17.

10. Quoted in Conrad Hyers, *The Comic Vision and the Christian Faith* (New York: Pilgrim Press, 1981), p. 50.

11. Quoted in Mary C. Boys, *Educating in Faith* (New York: Harper and Row, 1989), p. 209.

12. Thomas Merton, *The Way of Chuang Tsu* (New York: New Directions, 1965), p. 128.

13. Nhat Hanh, *Breath*, p. 4.

14. D. T. Suzuki, *Mysticism: Christian and Buddhist* (Westport, Conn.: Greenwood Press, 1975), pp. 45f.

15. Thomas Merton, *Raids on the Unspeakable* (New York: New Directions, 1966), p. 13.

16. Ibid., p. 14.

17. Thich Nhat Hanh, *The Miracle of Mindfulness* (Berkeley: Parallax Press, 1987), p. 30.

18. Thich Nhat Hanh, *The Heart of Understanding* (Berkeley: Parallax Press, 1988), p. 39.

19. Shunryu Suzuki, *Zen Mind, Beginner's Mind* (New York: Walker/Weather Hill, 1970), p. 89.

20. Ibid.

21. D. T. Suzuki, *Mysticism*, pp. 41f.

22. Abraham J. Heschel, *The Sabbath* (New York: Farrar, Strauss and Young, 1951), p. 36.

23. Quoted in D. T. Suzuki, *Mysticism*, p. 2.

24. Merton, *Raids*, p. 16.

25. D.T. Suzuki, *Mysticism*, p.46.

26. Dom Aelred Graham, *Zen Catholicism* (New York: Harcourt, Brace, and World, 1963), p. 23.

27. Merton, *Chuang Tsu*, p. 128.

28. Thich Nhat Hanh, *Being Peace* (Berkeley: Parallax Press, 1988), pp. 3f.

29. S. Suzuki, *Zen Mind*, p.115.

30. Ibid., p. 57.

31. Merton, *Chuang Tsu*, p. 141.

32. Nhat Hanh, *Peace*, p. 111.

33. Merton, *New Seeds*, p. 11.

34. Nhat Hanh, *Breath*, p. 57.

35. Nhat Hanh, *Mindfulness*, p. 14.

36. Quoted in D. T. Suzuki, *Mysticism*, p. 11.

37. Quoted in Matthew Fox, *Original Blessing* (Santa Fe, N.Mex.: Bear, 1983), p. 133.

38. Merton, *Chuang Tsu*, p. 80.

39. Parker Palmer, *To Know as We Are Known* (San Francisco: Harper and Row, 1983), p. 121.

40. Paul Tillich, *The Eternal Now* (New York: Scribner, 1963), p. 24.

41. Karl Rahner, *Encounters With Silence* (Westminster, Md.: Newman Press, 1960), p. 48.

42. Heschel, *Wonder*, p. 21.

43. D.T. Suzuki, *Mysticism*, p. 81.

44. Nhat Hanh, *Heart*, pp. 16f.
45. Nhat Hanh, *Peace*, p.48.
46. Graef, "A Hair," p. 184.
47. Nhat Hanh, *Peace*, p. 48.
48. Taisen Deshimaru, *Questions to a Zen Master* (New York: Dutton, 1985), p. 33.
49. Johannes B. Metz, *Theology of the World* (London: Burns and Oates, 1969), p. 104.
50. D. T. Suzuki, *Essays in Zen Buddhism* (New York: Grove Press, 1961), p. 319.
51. Paul Tillich, *History of Christian Thought* (New York: Harper and Row, 1968), p. 201.
52. Quoted in Fox, *Blessing*, p. 237.
53. Heschel, *Wonder*, p. 23.
54. Rainer Maria Rilke, quoted in David Stendl-Rast, *Gratefulness, the Heart of Prayer* (Ramsey, N.J.: Paulist Press, 1984), p. 30.

CHAPTER TWO

1. Thomas H. Groome, *Sharing Faith* (San Francisco: Harper San Francisco, 1991), p. 11.
2. Kathleen R. Fischer and Thomas N. Hart, *Christian Foundations* (New York: Paulist Press, 1986), p. 196.
3. Gabriel Moran, *Interplay: A Theory of Religion and Education* (Winona, MN: St. Mary's, 1981) p. 143.
4. Ibid., p. 193.
5. Moran, "The Ambiguities of Professionalization," in *Professional Approaches for Christian Educators*, Volume 9 (1978), p. 2.
6. Moran, *No Ladder*, pp. 13-14.
7. Ibid., p. 177.
8. This idea recurs often in Moran's writings, for example in *Religious Education Development*, as well as in the chapter on "Religious Education for Justice" in *Interplay: A Theory of Religion and Education*.
9. Gabriel Moran, *Religious Education Development* (Minneapolis: Winston Press, 1983), p. 102.
10. Ibid., p. 165.
11. Ibid., p. 207.
12. Ibid., p. 104.
13. Moran, *Interplay*, p. 129.
14. Gustavo Gutiérrez, *We Drink From Our Own Wells* (Maryknoll, N.Y.: Orbis Press, 1984), p. 32.
15. Ibid., pp. 41f.
16. Gustavo Gutiérrez, *On Job: God Talk and the Suffering of the Innocent* (Maryknoll, N.Y.: Orbis Press, 1987), p. 3.

17. Quoted in *Face to Face: The Bulletin of the Anti-Defamation League* (Spring, 1988).

18. Supercessionism is the anti-Jewish Christian perspective in which Judaism is understood, perfected in, and therefore replaced or superseded by Christianity.

19. *National Catholic Reporter* (November 11, 1988).

20. Heschel, *Wonder*, p. 28.

21. Martin Buber, *On Judaism* (New York: Schoken Books, 1967), p. 140.

22. Heschel, *Wonder*, p. 3.

23. Quoted in Gabriel Moran, "The Religious Element in Education," *The Living Light*, Volume 20, Number 4 (June 1984), p. 232.

24. Jack Spiro, "Form and Process in Jewish Tradition," *Religious Education*, Volume 82, Number 4 (Fall 1987), p. 547.

25. Ibid.

26. Abraham J. Heschel, *The Prophets*, Volume 1 (New York: Harper and Row, 1969), p. 19.

27. George Leonard, *Education and Ecstacy* (Berkeley, CA: North Atlantic, 1987), p. 26.

28. Paul Tillich, "Theology of Education," in *Theology and Culture* (New York: Oxford University Press, 1959), pp. 146-55.

29. Boys, *Educating*, pp. 3–110.

30. Ibid., p. 193.

31. Henri Giroux, *Ideology, Culture, and the Process of Schooling* (Philadelphia: Temple University Press, 1981) pp. 9ff.

32. Avery Dulles, *Models of the Church* (Garden City, N.Y.: Doubleday, 1974). He designates these facets of the church but does not speak of them as necessarily conflicting.

33. See Max Weber, *A Sociology of Religion* (Boston: Beacon Press, 1963).

34. See Ernst Troelstch, *The Social Teachings of the Christian Church* (New York: Macmillian, 1931), in five volumes.

35. David Hollenbach has an excellent discussion of the triumphal church and the shift to a servant model in the "Constitution on the Church in the Modern World of Vatican Council II" in chapters 1 and 2 of his book, *Justice Peace and Human Rights: American Catholic Social Ethics in a Pluralist Context* (New York: Crossroads, 1988).

36. For example, Adolph von Harnack, *What is Christianity?* (New York: Harper, 1957).

37. Paul Tillich, "The Spiritual Presence," *Systematic Theology*, Volume III, Chapter 2 (Chicago: University of Chicago Press, 1967).

38. Karl Rahner, *The Shape of the Church to Come* (New York: Seabury Press, 1974), pp. 26f.

39. Rahner, quoted in Richard P. McBrien, *Catholicism*, Volume 1 (Minneapolis: Winston Press, 1980), p. 148.

40. Ibid., p. 160.

41. Langdon Gilkey, *Catholicism Confronts Modernity* (New York: Seabury Press, 1975), p. 20.

42. Rosemary Haughton, *The Catholic Thing* (Springfield, Ill.: Templegate, 1979), p. 9.

43. Karl Rahner, *The Practice of Faith* (New York: Crossroad, 1983), p. 7.

CHAPTER THREE

1. Quoted in Maria Harris, *Teaching and Religious Imagination* (San Francisco: Harper and Row, 1987), p. 32.

2. Graef, "A Hair," p.174.

3. Quoted in Boys, *Educating*, p. 163.

4. Some of the authors whose work is surveyed in this chapter understand themselves to be religious educators; others might not identify themselves as such but are influential in religious education.

5. Merton, *Chuang Tsu*, p. 65.

6. Quoted in Luther Askeland, "The God in the Moment," *Cross Currents*, Volume 40, Number 4 (1991), p. 458.

7. Nhat Hanh, *Peace*, p. 64.

8. Merton, *Chuang Tsu*, p. 40.

9. Quoted in Fox, *Blessing*, p. 187.

10. James Fowler, *Becoming Adult, Becoming Christian* (San Francisco: Harper and Row, 1984), p. 62.

11. John Westerhoff, *Building God's People in a Materialist Society* (New York: Seabury Press, 1983), pp. 98f.

12. Thomas Del Prete, "Thomas Merton, Sincerity in Teaching," *Professional Approaches for Christian Educators*, Volume 20 (October 1990), p. 4. Emphasis mine. (This essay is drawn from Del Prete's book; see below).

13. Ibid., p. 5.

14. Westerhoff, *Building*, p. 109.

15. Del Prete, "Sincerity," p. 4.

16. Palmer, *To Know*, p. 13.

17. Fowler, *Adult*, p. 147.

18. Craig Dykstra, *Vision and Character* (New York: Paulist Press, 1981), pp. 95ff.

19. Palmer, *To Know*, pp. 67f.

20. Fowler, *Adult*, pp. 64f

21. Thomas Del Prete, *Thomas Merton and the Education of the Whole Person* (Birmingham, Ala.: Religious Education Press, 1990), p. 44.

22. S. Suzuki, *Zen Mind*, p. 126.

23. Ibid., p. 121.

24. Westerhoff, *Building*, p. 99.

25. Ibid., p. 108.

26. Del Prete, *Thomas Merton*, p. 97.

27. Fowler, *Adult*, pp. 68, 70.

28. Maria Harris, *Religious Imagination*, pp. 24f.

29. Since this section is a detailed analysis of a chapter from one of Maria Harris' books with many quotations, individual endnotes will not appear. All quotations are from chapter 2, "Teaching," pp. 23-40 in Harris, *Religious Imagination*.

30. Palmer, *To Know*, p. 8.

31. Quoted in Fox, *Blessing*, p. 84.

32. Ibid., p. 193.

33. Merton, *New Seeds*, p. 297.

34. Nhat Hanh, *The Sun*, p. 48. Emphasis mine.

35. Donald Gray, "Patience: Human and Divine," *Cross Currents* (Winter 1975), pp. 410f.

36. Gabriel Moran, *Religious Body* (New York: Seabury Press, 1974), pp. 86-87.

37. Moran, *RED*, p. 155.

38. Ibid., pp. 140f.

39. Ibid., p. 181.

40. D. T. Suzuki, *Essays*, p. 1.

41. Moran, *RED*, p. 141.

42. Gabriel Moran, *Education Toward Adulthood* (New York: Paulist Press, 1979), p. 72.

43. Moran, *Body*, p. 97. Emphasis mine.

44. Moran, *RED*, p. 155.

45. Moran, *No Ladder*, pp. 61, 63. Emphasis mine.

46. Ibid., pp. 63f.

47. Moran, *Body*, p. 139.

48. Moran, *Adulthood*, p. 73.

49. Moran, *Body*, pp. 105-6.

50. Moran, *No Ladder*, p. 177.

CHAPTER FOUR

1. Cited in Dick Westley, *Theology of Presence* (Mystic, Conn.: Twenty-Third Publications, 1988), pp. 80-83.

2. Cited in Dorothee Sölle, *To Work and to Love* (Philadelphia: Fortress Press, 1984), p. 84.

3. Ibid., p. 2.

4. Westley, *Theology*, p. 82.

5. Peter Berger (ed.), *The Human Shape of Work* (New York: Macmillan, 1964), pp. 218f.

6. C. S. Lewis, *The ScrewTape Letters* (New York: Macmillan, 1943), p. 7.

7. Cited in Hyers, *Comic Vision*, p. 26.

8. Merton, *Chuang Tsu*, p. 44.

9. Heschel, *Sabbath*, p. 13.

10. Ibid., p. 22.

11. D. T. Suzuki, *An Introduction to Zen Buddhism* (New York: Grove Press, 1964), p. 58.

12. Katsuki Sekida, *Zen Training* (New York: Weather Hill, 1985), p. 158.

13. John Julian Ryan, *The Humanization of Man* (New York: Newman Press, 1972), p. 40.

14. Ibid., p. 36.

15. Ibid., p. 41.

16. Ibid., p. 36.

17. Berger, *Work*, p. 222.

18. Ibid.

19. Quoted in Stanley Parker, *Leisure and Work* (London: Allen and Unwin, 1983), pp.84f.

20. Joseph Pieper, *Leisure, the Basis of Culture* (New York: Pantheon Books, 1952), p. 38.

21. Ibid. See also Monica Furlong's wonderful chapter on the seven deadly sins in *Christian Uncertainties* (Cambridge, Mass.: Cowley Publications, 1982).

22. Sölle, *To Work*, pp. 56f.

23. Berger, *Work*, p. 224.

24. In Gideon Goosen, *The Theology of Work* (Hales Corners, Wis.: Clergy Book Service, 1974), p. 62.

25. Berger, *Work*, p. 223. I am indebted to Peter Berger for this review of certain features of classical sociology of work.

26. Robert Howard, *Brave New Workplace* (New York: Viking, 1985), pp. 5f.

27. Ibid., quoting Robert Reich, pp. 6f.

28. Ibid., p. 9.

29. Herbert Marcuse, *One Dimensional Man* (Boston: Beacon Press, 1964), pp. xiii, xv.

30. Ruth M. Goohill (ed.), *The Wisdom of Rabbi Heschel* (New York: Charles Scribner, 1976), p. 86.

31. Ibid., p. 93.

32. From a 1972 television broadcast of an interview with Rabbi Heschel by Carl Stern.

33. Pope John Paul II, *On Human Work* (Boston: St. Paul's Editions, 1982), p. 39.

34. Hyers, *Comic Vision*, p. 32.

35. Ibid., pp. 33ff.

36. Ibid., p. 94.

37. Ibid., p. 95.

38. Moran, *Interplay*, pp. 138-39.

39. Moran, *RED*, p. 180.

40. Ibid., p. 206

41. Ibid., p. 180

42. Pierre Teilhard de Chardin, *The Divine Milieu* (New York: Harper and Row, 1968), p. 55.

43. Ibid., p. 56.

44. Philip Kapleau, *Three Pillars of Zen* (New York: Harper and Row, 1965), p. 211.

45. Heschel, *Book*, p. 73.

46. Merton, *Chuang Tsu*, p. 152.

47. Sunyana Graef, "The Foundations of Ecology in Zen Buddhism," *Religious Education*, Volume 85, Number 1 (Winter 1990), p. 44.

48. D.T. Suzuki, *Essays*, p. 319.

49. S. Suzuki, *Zen Mind*, p. 22.

50. Sölle, *To Work*, p. 62.

51. Teilhard de Chardin, *Divine Milieu*, p. 56.

52. S. Suzuki, *Zen Mind*, pp. 27, 53.

53. Merton, *Raids*, pp. 21-22.

54. Sölle, *To Work*, p. 57.

55. Nhat Hanh, *Mindfulness*, pp. 2ff. Emphasis mine.

56. Goosen, *Theology*, p. 55.

57. Sölle, *To Work*, pp. 66, 77.

58. Parker, *To Know*, p. 15.

59. Francis Schüssler Fiorenza, in Gregory Baum (ed.), *Work and Religion* (New York: Seabury Press, 1980), p. 96.

60. Joe Holland, *Creative Communion: Toward a Spirituality of Work* (New York, Paulist Press, 1989), p. 29.

61. Heschel, *Wonder*, p. 46.

62. I justify exclusive interest in this paper in the work of adults since I believe that more youthful workers, youth and young adults, are less likely, and in fewer numbers, to experience their work related frustrations and limitations as requiring irony and contemplation.

63. Moran, *RED*, p. 171

64. Ibid., p. 193.

65. Marjorie Fisk Lowenthal, *Four Stages of Life* (San Francisco: Jossey-Bass, 1975), p. 220.

66. Moran, *RED*, p. 87.

67. Ibid., p. 181.

68. Ibid., p. 88.

69. Parker Palmer, *The Active Life* (San Francisco: Harper and Row, 1990), p. 66.

70. Moran, *Interplay*, p. 87.

71. Quoted in Parker, *Leisure*, p. 115.

72. Ibid., pp. 80ff.

73. Cited in Joseph Campbell with Bill Moyers, *The Power of Myth* (New York: Doubleday, 1988), p. 86.

74. Ernest Becker, *The Denial of Death* (New York: Free Press, 1973), p. 317. I am grateful to Dick Westley for knowledge of Becker's and the subsequent Heschel statement on heroism, cf. *Morality and Its Beyond*, p. 20.

75. Abraham J. Heschel, *Who is Man?* (Stanford, Calif.: Stanford University Press, 1965), p. 35.

76. Hyers, *Comic Vision*, p. 147.

77. Merton, *New Seeds*, p. 296.

78. Nhat Hanh, *Peace*, p. 86.

CHAPTER FIVE

1. Wendy Wright, *Sacred Dwellings: A Spirituality of Family Life* (New York: Crossroad, 1989), p. 65.

2. W. Robert Beavers and Robert B. Hampson, *Successful Families* (New York: Norton, 1990), p. 51.

3. *Oxford Dictionary of Quotations*, Third Edition (Oxford: Oxford University Press, 1983), p. 118.

4. Maria Harris, *Fashion Me a People* (Louisville, Ky.: Westminster/John Knox Press, 1989), p. 87. Emphasis mine.

5. Quoted in Reinhold Niebuhr, *The Nature and Destiny of Man*, Volume I (New York: Scribner, 1964), p. 157.

6. Beavers and Hampson, *Successful*, p. 51.

7. Westley, *Theology*, p. 17.

8. Ernest Boyer, Jr., *A Way in the World: Family Life as Spiritual Discipline* (San Francisco: Harper and Row), p. 21.

9. Furlong, *Uncertainties*, p. 17.

10. For example, Stanley Hauerwas, "The Family as a School for Character," *Religious Education*, Volume 80, Number 2 (Spring 1985), pp. 273-285.

11. Quoted in Mark Poster, *Critical Theory of the Family* (New York: Seabury Press, 1978), p. 14.

12. Wright, *Sacred*, pp. 20ff.
13. Mary Perkins Ryan, *Beginning at Home* (Collegeville, Minn.: Liturgical Press, 1955), p. 112. Emphasis mine.
14. Wright, *Sacred*, p. 24.
15. Beavers and Hampson, *Successful*, p. 48.
16. Nhat Hanh, *Peace*, pp. 35f.
17. Quoted from *How to Help Your Child Have a Spiritual Life* in Roberta Nelson, "Parents as Resident Theologians," *Religious Education*, Volume 83, Number 4 (Fall 1988), p. 492. Emphasis mine.
18. Furlong, *Uncertainties*, p. 17. Emphasis mine.
19. Quoted in Stanley L. Saxton, Patricia Voydanoff and Angela Zukowski (eds.), *The Changing Family* (Chicago: Loyola University Press, 1984), p. 49. Emphasis mine.
20. Francis De Sales, *An Introduction to the Devout Life* (Garden City, N.Y.: Image Books, 1972), p. 8.
21. Ibid.
22. R. S. Peters, "Concrete Principles and Rational Passions," in Theodore and Nancy Sizer (eds.), *Moral Education: Five Lectures* (Cambridge, Mass.: Harvard University Press, 1970), p. 36.
23. Quoted from "Authority and the Family," in Poster, *Critical Theory*, p. 54.
24. Quoted in Hyers, *Comic Vision*, p. 13.
25. Ralph Waldo Emerson.
26. Henry Nelson Wieman, *Religious Experience and Scientific Method* (Westport, Conn.: Greenwood Press, 1970), p. 69.
27. Edward Robinson, *The Original Vision* (Oxford: The Religious Experience Research Unit, 1977), p. 9.
28. Jerome Berryman, "Teaching as Presence and the Existential Curriculum," *Religious Education*, Volume 85, Number 4 (Fall, 1990), p. 509.
29. Moran, *RED*, p. 188.
30. Quoted from *Orthodoxy* in Moran, *RED*, p. 147.
31. Heschel, *Wonder*, p. 3.
32. Quoted in Goohill, *Wisdom of Heschel*, p. 141.
33. Moran, *RED*, p. 188
34. Berryman, "Teaching as Presence," pp. 510, 527.
35. Quoted in Moran, *RED*, p. 177
36. Hyers, *Comic Vision*, p. 13.
37. Moran, *RED*, p. 188.
38. Quoted in Hyers, *Comic Vision*, p. 24.
39. Ibid., p. 25.
40. Ibid., p. 38.
41. Ibid., p. 8.

42. Quoted in Charles Shelton, *Adolescent Spirituality* (Chicago: Loyola University Press, 1983), p. 2.

43. Erik Erikson, *Insight and Responsibility* (New York: W. W. Norton, 1964), p. 90.

44. Padraic O'Hare, "Hospitality as Paradigm for Youth Ministry," *Journal of Youth Ministry*, Volume II, Number 2 (Summer 1984), pp. 3-12.

45. Wright, *Sacred*, pp. 33, 36.

46. Erikson, *Insight*, p. 125.

47. Gisela Konopka, *Young Girls: A Portrait of Adolescence* (Englewood Cliffs, N.J.: Prentice-Hall, 1976), p. 2.

48. Charlotte Kahn, "I Am That I Am: A Psychology of Teenage Jewish Identity," in *Religious Education*, Volume 75, Number 3 (May-June 1980), p. 356.

49. Maria Harris, *Portrait of Youth Ministry* (New York: Paulist Press, 1981), p. 119.

50. Moran, *RED*, pp. 179f.

51. Goohill, *Wisdom of Heschel*, p. 80.

52. Erikson, *Insight*, p. 126.

53. John Westerhoff, *Will Our Children Have Faith?* (New York: Seabury Press, 1976), pp. 89ff.

54. Sharon Parks, *The Critical Years* (San Francisco: Harper and Row, 1986), p. 199.

55. Goohill, *Wisdom of Heschel*, p. 89.

56. Johannes B. Metz, *The Emergent Church* (New York: Crossroad, 1981), p. 8.

57. Quoted in John Shea, O.S.A., "The Emergence of a Sense of Self: The Transition from Late Adolescence into Young Adulthood," in *Journal of Youth Ministry*, Volume II, Number 2 (Summer 1984), p. 15.

58. Moran, *RED*, p. 205.

59. Quoted in Walter Kaufman (ed.), *The Portable Neitzsche* (New York: Viking Press, 1954), pp. 138f.

60. Quoted in Shea, "Emergence of a Sense," p. 16.

61. Ibid., p. 20.

62. Moran, *RED*, p. 205.

63. Nhat Hanh, *Peace*, pp. 83–102.

64. Kaufman, *Portable*, p. 139.

65. James and Kathleen McGinnis, "'Peace-ing it Together': Family Religious Education for Peace," *Religious Education*, Volume 83, Number 4 (Fall 1988), pp. 532–45.

66. James and Kathleen McGinnis, *Parenting For Peace and Justice*, First Edition (Maryknoll, N.Y.: Orbis Press, 1981), pp. 116f.

67. Harris, *Fashion*, pp. 86f.

68. Graef, "Foundations," p. 44.
69. Wright, *Sacred*, p. 182.
70. Ibid., pp. 88, 90, 105, 116.
71. Ibid., p. 146.
72. Ibid., pp. 197f.
73. Moran, *RED*, pp. 192f.
74. Boyer, *A Way*, p. 84.

CHAPTER SIX

1. Karl Rahner, "How to Receive a Sacrament and Mean It," *Theological Digest*, Volume 19, Number 3 (Autumn 1971), p. 97.
2. Heschel, *Wonder*, p. 22.
3. S. Suzuki, *Zen Mind*, pp. 30, 27.
4. Thomas Keating, *The Heart of the World* (New York: Crossroads, 1981), p. 1.
5. Thomas Keating, Basil Pennington, Thomas Clark, *Finding Grace at the Center* (Still River, Mass.: St. Bede Publications, 1978), pp. 12-18.
6. Nhat Hanh, *Breath*, p. 8.
7. Nhat Hanh, *Peace*, pp. 45f.
8. Moran, *No Ladder*, p. 63. Emphasis mine.

EPILOGUE

1. Robert Bellah, Richard Madsen, et al., *The Good Society* (New York: Alfred A. Knopf, 1991), p. 254.
2. Martin Buber, *I and Thou* (New York, Scribner, 1970), p. 167.

APPENDIX

1. Readers are urged to avoid unsophisticated and exegetically uniformed treatment of passages in which scribes and pharisees are excoriated. Carrying these verses into contemporary Christian religious education as if they were as "true" as elemental features of Jesus' teaching, ministry, and witness, with little understanding of the context of polemics within the Matthean community against the Jews who did not accept Jesus, is an especially violent use of scripture. For help in reforming anti-Jewish attitudes read Leon Klenicki and Eugene J. Fisher, *Roots and Branches: Biblical Judaism, Rabbinic Judaism and*

Early Christianity, originally a *PACE* monograph, now available through the Anti-Defamation League.

2. See Gustavo Gutiérrez, *On Job: God Talk and the Suffering of the Innocent*. This powerful study of the Book of Job contains the extraordinary interpretation of Job as experiencing a contemplative breakthrough precisely as he gives up trying to lay hands on God, in the sense of applying rationalistic categories of cause-and-effect thinking to divine power. There is no final answer to the question of theodicy. But when Job says that up till now he has only heard about God and that now he sees God, Gutiérrez maintains he is a contemplative being who can celebrate. Even in suffering he will not be sorrowful, the ultimate quality of contemplation.

3. Shunryu Suzuki's simple but eloquent summary of the life of Zen can serve well as a Christian *gatha*: " In order to exist in the realm of Buddha nature [Christ nature], it is necessary to die as a small being moment by moment."

Index

163